The Abnormal Journey

4 PILLARS OF FINANCIAL SUCCESS

BY NICK PAGANO

Primo-
Be Abnormal!

Nick P

MAR 2013

This book is dedicated to those who want more of their life and are willing to do something about it!

Welcome to the Abnormal Journey!

ACKNOWLEDGMENTS

The book of Ecclesiastes in the Bible states "There is nothing new under the sun". I agree with that statement and the book you are holding and the journey that is contained is not new. The information presented here is not new. The idea of people improving their lives with the power of the mind and a commitment to do so is an age-old human endeavor. No one ever succeeds alone, and the development of this book is no exception.

I have many people to thank for their assistance in helping this project come to fruition. Some of them I know and have worked with personally; others have helped from afar by allowing me to read their books and listen to their messages.

First and foremost I want to thank my family, Janice, Nicholas and Colton for their support, flexibility, and encouragement to get this project completed. Secondly, I need to thank Tammy and Julie who served as my literary team and offered brilliant insights and brainstorming. I also need to thank some of my business partners that shared their insights over the years- Demond Crump, Melissa Boston, Scott Tomer, Ken Hubbard and Lloyd Tomer.

Finally, I feel the need to thank and acknowledge a host of authors and speakers who have had an impact on my thinking. Men such as Robert Kiyosaki, Harv Eker, the late Jim Rohn, Daniel Pink, Paul Zane Pilzer, and others whose works have challenged and inspired me.

CONTENTS

INTRODUCTION

Do the rich get richer? Almost everyone agrees that they do. But let's ask the next question. Why? In this story we are going to explore this question through the eyes of Larry and Sara. Larry and Sara have the same issues that many in America experience. They are not sure if they have enough money to raise and educate their children. They are not sure if they will be able to retire and they are not confident that they are making the financial progress they had hoped to make. They are frustrated and this frustration leads them to seek some answers. Through a fortuitous encounter, our characters meet and develop a relationship with an older couple who is willing to help them along their journey to gain financial knowledge and ultimately financial success.

Many of us find ourselves in a similar situation as Larry and Sara. We wonder if the path we are on is going to work. We look for a simple answer or some kind of an advantage. We look for anyone who would be willing to help us. We live in a time where the "tried and true" economic rules do not seem to apply, or at least the rules need to be modified. *It takes money to make money*, is violated by numerous billionaires with stories of small beginnings; *you can't lose money in real estate* is violated everyday to the financial horror of hundreds if not thousands. *Your home is your biggest and best investment* has created a lot of trepidation and fear because of what has become phantom equity. One report released by The Joint Economic Committee estimated $71 billion in housing wealth will be destroyed and States will lose $917 million in property tax revenue because of foreclosures[1]. It seems everywhere we look the economic news and outlook is bleak. If we simply keep doing the same old things over and over again but expect different results, Albert Einstein defines us as insane.

It is my hope that this story and the concepts outlined can help you on your road to financial success. There are only two ways you can leave this message: changed or resigned. You can either take 100 percent responsibility for changing the financial course of your life, or you will resign yourself to staying with the 95 percent who are headed for financial failure. It is up to you. Only you can decide your future. Please don't put your head under the pillow and pretend things will somehow sort themselves out. A lot of people live their lives with the *we will just see what happens attitude*. For most that approach simply will not work. You must take action. That is a REALITY. Life is simply a matter of choices. Nothing forces us to be who we are or where we end up in life. Each individual choice that we have made has placed us exactly where we are in this moment in time. Bad things happen, but even these offer us a choice of how we will respond and react.

If you are not happy with where you are or where you are going – CHOOSE TO CHANGE. It really is that simple. You have probably heard the old Chinese proverb: *The journey of a thousand miles begins with the first step.* The first step is choosing, choose to change.

The Abnormal Journey is the result of a lifetime of observation and reflection about the economic situation that we live in. It seems to me that most Americans strive to live *normal* lives. But let's explore what is considered *normal* in today's culture. It is *normal* to have a job. It is *normal* to be middle class, not necessarily to be rich. It is *normal* to work hard, get a tax refund, and work well into your 60's or even 70's. It is *normal* to make less than $200,000 per year and live paycheck to paycheck; as many as 77% of Americans do.[2]   It is *normal* to be busier than ever before, and save less than 1% of your income. According to MSN Money, "The United States is on track to record a savings rate for the year below 1%, which would be the lowest since the depths of the Great Depression, when the rate turned negative." [3]

My story is similar to Larry's and probably yours. I had always followed the advice of the infamous *they*. Go to school (did it), get good grades (did it), get a good job (did it), work overtime (did it) and prove your loyalty and commitment (did it). Then I looked around one day and realized that I was falling behind and there were a lot of people following the rules and ending up falling short with me. I decided I did not want to be one of them, living a *normal* life seemed to invite financial challenges. In this book you will find 4 pillars that I have discovered the hard way. I am the first to admit that I am still continuing to learn and apply them. Now that I have started, I changed the course of my life which has allowed me to recognize and take advantage of whole a new set of opportunities.

Thomas Edison once said: "Opportunity is missed by most people because it is dressed in overalls and looks like work". I challenge you to renew your mind and allow yourself to quit operating on the wrong side of truths. Robert Frost wrote about two roads. When I personally "took the one less traveled" it has "made all the difference in the world".

I hope this book challenges you to take the road less traveled. I challenge you to get rid of any attitude allowing you to *settle for* only what you have known. Find something inside of yourself that drives you to *know* that there is a better way and that you deserve it. I hope this book challenges you to *choose* to do it the right way as you move into the future. Further more, I hope you recognize the positive power of being ABNORMAL!

CHAPTER 1

THE JOURNEY BEGINS

Great spirits have always encountered violent opposition from mediocre minds. – Albert Einstein

Larry was living the American dream. He had done everything his dad had taught him to do. He married his high school sweetheart. He had a couple of kids. He voted in every election. He and his wife Sara even volunteered at the local senior citizen center. Larry had worked at one company his entire life, saved for a rainy day and invested in the company stock. Yet somehow his American dream had evolved into an American nightmare.

Questions swirled in his head. How did he get here? Where had all the money gone? Was he doing something wrong? Did he lose the directions to easy street? More importantly, what should he do? He could blame the economy, the politicians, or even blame himself, however placing blame would not change the circumstances. Besides, he did not feel that he was to blame; he had led a good, hard-working life. He always picked up the overtime when it was offered. He had saved for the kid's college. He had put money in his 401K. He had even bought a rental house. He refinanced his house to get a lower interest rate. He didn't live extravagantly. But now he found himself wondering why his life and dreams for financial success were not working. He felt inadequate as if he was just middle aged, living in Middle America, right in the middle of middle class. Maybe the rules had somehow changed and he did not get the email.

None of his friends were experiencing the same problems. Or were they? Come to think of it, he hadn't been asked by the Curtis' to pick up their mail while they went on the annual vacation. His long time neighbors, the Bradley's, hadn't asked him to watch Rufus their pet spaniel. He hadn't even been subjected to the annual *home movie night* to view the Carmichael's yearly adventures.

As he reflected on his situation, a startling thought crossed his mind. Who or where do you go to get an assessment and advice? He couldn't go to his parents; their financial situation appeared to be roughly the same as his. Talking with his wife Sara would just scare her. His best friend worked at the same place and struggled with the same issues. He didn't have a real accountant or lawyer. Even if he did, they would charge for the advice anyway. He went to the computer and typed *financial advice* into Google and got 77,000,000 hits. Where should he start? His pastor's most recent sermon was about the evils of having money.

His financial planner was always pitching this deal or that, and he didn't seem to have that much more of a *life* than he had. The library and bookstores seemed to have a proliferation of financial and self help books, but in his heart he didn't feel that was what he needed. Maybe there was a dummy book on the subject, because that was exactly how he was feeling at this moment. He knew there were help groups for alcoholics and gamblers, but what about *normal* people who didn't know what their problems were, so they did not know how to categorize or discuss them? He read somewhere that over 90% of Americans retired broke. Obviously, he did not want that.

Larry decided to go for a walk. Maybe he just needed some fresh air and exercise. Watching TV was not going to solve anything. It seemed to him that all the commercials were about drugs which had more hideous side effects than the problems they supposedly solved. He did see that one financial commercial, with the fellow walking around with a number over his head. The number was supposed to represent the amount he was looking for in order to retire. The commercial goes on to show his neighbor with his number, which read *gazillion*. What was it he said, something about him just throwing money at it? That wasn't what he was doing; was it? Perhaps he needed to rethink that.

Larry felt that he had done all that he had known to do, all that he had been taught to do to realize the American dream, all the *normal things*. Why wasn't it working? What if *normal* people didn't really want to discover how to make and keep more money? That made startling sense to him. If *they* couldn't tell him how to make more money and pay less, then perhaps he should not listen to or do what *they* said to do. He began to ask himself, what is *normal*? *Normal* people had jobs. After all, the government always based the state of the economy by reporting the number of people that were out of work, the unemployment rate. Furthermore, almost all the people he and Sara knew had jobs, so it must be *normal*, right?

As he pondered this, a new thought entered his mind, one that he had never had before. Were any of these *normal* people significantly better off than Sara and he are? Was it *normal* to be rich; was it *normal* to want to be rich? Was it *normal to* get two weeks off per year for vacation? Was it *normal to* live paycheck to paycheck?

The summer sun and air had its intended effects and soon he started feeling better. But the questions were still there, gnawing at him. Was his *financial plan* working? He felt like he had more month than money. Then a new and terrifying thought crossed his mind. What if he outlives his money? Was that possible? He had heard stories about senior citizens eating dog and cat food. Yuck! How did they get to that point in their lives? Was his life moving in the same direction?

The more he thought the more he realized that he had more questions than he had answers. His thoughts had taken him in a full circle but now he was motivated to find out where he might go to get some answers. He didn't have a crystal ball, but there had to be answers for his financial future somewhere. Larry resolved to find them.

When he got home he told Sara of his mission to find answers to his questions. Ever the supportive spouse, she encouraged the exercise and agreed to help. She knew there was more to life than the way they were living it. She knew that it may not be easy, but she already had some ideas to begin the search. She told Larry that she had recently overheard one of the ladies at the hair salon make the comment "it seems that the rich are always getting richer." She suggested that they start there. They could start by talking to someone who is rich. After a lengthy discussion, they discovered that they didn't know any *rich people*. They didn't know any professional athletes, rock stars, movie stars, internet millionaires or lottery winners. Certainly, there was no one in their family or in their immediate group of friends. They agreed that talking to someone rich was a good start, but they would have to think about who that someone was.

Monday at work Larry felt like a different person. He walked taller. He walked faster. He felt his life had purpose. Over lunch in the cafeteria, he shared his new found mission with a few of his coworkers. He was shocked by their perspectives and comments. "You will never be rich", one said. "Money is not that important, besides, it is the root of all evil", said another. A third shared that "All rich people are miserable and greedy, why would you want to be rich?" That certainly wasn't the reception he was expecting.

He couldn't wait to get home to find out if Sara had any more luck or a better reception than he had. Over dinner Sara reported, "I spoke with two people today and got two totally different answers. My mom just said, 'you and Larry are doing fine, why mess it up?' After seeing mom, I stopped in at the coffee shop and while I was there, a woman came up to me out of the blue and asked if I was OK. I told her I was, but she asked if she could join me and I agreed. After we talked for a while, I shared with her our new journey. Her perspective was totally different than my mom's. She encouraged me and told me to go for it. We spent the next couple of hours talking and she had some great comments. Here, I wrote them down."

"Wait a second, who is this woman?"

"Her name is Miss Chris and she gave me her card,"

He looked over the card, "It doesn't have a company name. Did she seem like a wacko?" He felt protective of Sara and did not know if he liked the idea of her sitting in the coffee shop talking over their own struggles with a stranger.

"No she seemed like a caring, insightful woman who could tell that I had something on my mind and actually went out of her way to offer to help. I am so glad that I decided to take advantage of the opportunity."

"Did she tell you she was rich? Did she wear a big ring? Did she drive a nice car?" He continued to question.

"I didn't notice her car."

"How do we know she isn't some wacko who hangs out at the coffee shop and gives people false hope?"

"I am surprised at you. I thought we were on this new road together and now it sounds like you aren't going to trust me to be on the same team. I believe that we should surround ourselves with wise people. I learned during my conversation with Miss Chris that she and her husband are very successful financial coaches and have been working and helping people for many years."

"I guess that makes sense," Larry conceded. "I guess I am disappointed because I thought my buddies would be excited and encouraging, but they all just jumped on the same bandwagon."

"Bandwagon?"

"You know the *you can't be rich* bandwagon. All the guys at the plant seem to be on it. They aren't rich and therefore no one else can be, including us. Anyway, let's take a look at what you wrote down."

"OK. First, she said that there are **4 Pillars of Financial Success.**

"I thought we just had to work hard, keep our nose to the grindstone, and do the best we can. But obviously that is not working out so well. I feel that the *rules* that I have followed my whole life don't work, and there are more rules I don't even know and I don't know where to find them."

"I agree, but I also believe that Miss Chris and her husband really may be able to help us. Are you willing to meet with them and learn more?"

"Yeah, let's do it."

"Great. Let's give her a call and schedule a time to meet with her and her husband."

CHAPTER 2
MINDSETS

We've got two lives, one we're given and the other one we make. -- Mary Chapin Carpenter, Hard Way

Fortunately, Miss Chris answered the phone right away. Sara started. "It was such a pleasure meeting you today. I have my husband Larry with me on speaker phone and we both really appreciate your willingness to meet with us."

"It is nice to meet you Larry. Really, it is my pleasure to meet and talk to you both," Miss Chris assured them. "My husband and I are committed to helping people shorten their learning curve and increase their income. We have been incredibly blessed and we believe it is our privileges to share what we have learned with any and everyone that is interested in learning. Perhaps it would make you a little more comfortable to know that we have been where I believe you currently are."

"Really? Um, well then exactly *how* can you help us? Sara told me that you were rich." Larry questioned with a touch of anger in his tone.

"I said, we *were* where you are. Ralph Waldo Emerson said, 'What lies behind us, and what lies before us are small matters compared to what lies within us.' My husband and I believe that financial independence and desire for wealth lies within everyone, including you."

They heard Miss Chris chuckle softly and continue, "Yes, we *were* where you are, until a friend of ours told us that creating wealth begins between the ears. It all starts with our mindset. It is simple and complicated at the same time. Complicated only because it is probably something you have not been taught and because you are going to go against the status quo, but it is easy once it has been mastered. I believe that we all have the basic ingredients inside; we just need to learn to unleash them. The sad thing is that most will never exercise those innate abilities so they are forced to live lives as HD Thoreau describes in *Walden: Most men lead lives of quiet desperation and go to the grave with the song still in them.* Call it resignation or desperation; I am describing most people's lives. They go with flow, doing what is expected of them in order to fit in and pay the bills without ever exploring what it is they truly want out of life. People are either willing to use the substance within them that yearns for self-direction and self-support or they are not. Only you can examine yourselves and answer this challenge."

Larry and Sara looked at each other. They had never heard anyone talk like this before. Something inside them was going to help them? They looked back to the speaker phone and Sara said, "Please continue, we want to hear more."

"In the late '80s my husband and I had to take the same inventory that I believe you two are now taking of yourselves and your lives. We had to be honest with ourselves about where our life was going, and where it was likely to end up. We had a growing business yet we knew, deep down inside, that if the income ever stopped, or even dipped significantly, our lifestyle would collapse. Like most Americans, we were living up to the maximum of our income and with the help of Uncle Visa and Aunt MasterCard, a little beyond our income."

Sara and Larry smiled at each other as they continued to listen.

"When we stared it right in the face, we knew it was a house of cards, no pun intended. We knew at that time that when our working years ran out, we would be in a real mess. Unfortunately, circumstances did not allow us much time to figure out what to do. Our business resold another company's product, and when that other company suddenly went out of business, it pulled us down with it."

"Is that when you started creating wealth? Tell us, how you started again, you said it begins between your ears," Larry questioned.

"Right you are. With all the people we work with, we have come to find that there are different mindsets and characteristics that make up those mindsets. We have seen a wealthy mindset, a worker mindset and a wisher mindset. It is our belief that the *only* difference between these mindsets is willingness and a decision to change. It is not a matter of age, education, race, or anything besides a decision to understand and know that there is a better way and then a decision to do what it takes to change. "

"I think we have already made a decision to change! What are the characteristics of the wealthy?" Sara said as she and Larry nodded to each other. They truly were excited to be talking about how they could change their circumstances.

"That is good news, you have already decided! That is the first step. I'll list the characteristics and we'll talk about which one you may fall into today, and which one you want to be.

The characteristics or the Wealthy Mindset include:
- o   OPTIMISTIC
- o   RISK TAKERS
- o   INVESTORS
- o   DREAMERS | VISIONARIES
- o   INNOVATIVE
- o   DECISIVE | COMMITTED

The characteristics of the Working Mindset:
- o   COMFORTABLE
- o   CONSERVATIVE

- SAVERS
- ANALYTICAL | RESEARCH
- 2 CLASS SOCIETY
- NO ACCOUNTABILITY

And the wishers- sometimes called whiners Mindset can be identified by:

- INSTANT GRATIFICATION
- NO VISION
- EASILY PERSUADED
- DREAM KILLER
- ENTITLEMENT MENTALITY
- COMFORT ZONE SPECIALIST
- AVOID INFORMATION

Larry and Sarah both thought they fell somewhere between the wishers and working mindsets. They looked at the characteristics of the wealthy and wondered if they would ever be able to describe themselves in that way. Investors? They barely had enough each month for the essentials, how could they invest? On the other hand, they may be Risk Takers. Here they were on the phone with a stranger discussing their finances. Finally Larry admitted, "Miss Chris, you have been so helpful and we are willing to have a wealthy mindset, but we don't today. How can we go from where we are to where we want to be? Does it take something special, something that we may not have? I mentioned my dreams to the guys I work with and they ridiculed me and my goals."

"Mindsets. Larry you shared your dreams with people that do not have the mindset of wealthy, so they will not understand and may even want you to stay where you are financially, so that they feel more comfortable with their circumstances. Perhaps I should explain a couple of things

13

to you about the journey you are about to embark on. There are success principles or laws just like there are physical principles and laws. These principles are always at work, just like the physical ones. It does not matter if you believe in gravity or not, gravity is a principle and is always at work. Whether you believe in gravity or not when you step off a cliff….."

"I still fall," Larry completed her sentence.

"Right you are. Well, there are principles for success as well. You asked if it takes something special to have a wealthy mindset. It does. It takes *action*. If you cannot make yourself *do* the things that could improve your life, your life will most likely end up the same as the other 95 percent of the financial failures in America. It is that simple. You can have the best opportunities, the best plans, and the best tools, but if you can't put all that into *action*, it is all wasted! And so is your life. What happens for most people is that they redefine success to be where they are. Then they begin to rationalize and justify their lives. The facts are compelling; the majority of Americans end up living in more of a nightmare than a dream. As a matter of fact, when we ask most people how they are doing, they reply 'fine' and they truly believe that their financial lives are fine. They live paycheck to paycheck, or sometimes spending over their paycheck, for their entire lives but still believe that retirement is going to be better, different and euphoric. This seems pretty self-evident, but most Americans just float through their financial life, hoping it will all just work out somehow. This is, of course, is a form of insanity. It will not work out. The federal statistics are staggering and prove that it does not work out for 95 percent of Americans, and it is the same in Canada. It will not work out unless you make it work out. But the problem most people face is that they can rarely think about getting ahead when they can hardly keep up. They dig a hole of debt, jump in, and then spend month after month dragging dirt in on themselves, wondering why they're getting financially buried. The fact that you need a financial plan to reach financial success is really not a secret. But most people don't know where to start. And that is where we would like to help you. Are you willing to let us?"

"Absolutely!" Larry and Sara both agreed.

"Why don't you come over for dinner on Friday evening and we'll begin. Our address in on the card and we'll see you around 6pm. My husband and I can go over the **4 PILLARS OF FINANCIAL SUCCESS**, we call them **4Ps**. The rich get richer because of these **4Ps**. Let me just summarize them for you quickly.

"First, the rich know different things, we call that the first **P: PRINCIPLE**. The second is that they think differently about life, money, and other things, we call that **PERSPECTIVE**. Thirdly, they do different things, we call that **PRACTICES.** And finally, they have different relationships, we call that **PEOPLE.** As you see I haven't mentioned birthrights. I haven't mentioned luck. I haven't mentioned education. Larry and Sara, I want you to think about the characteristics of the wealthy mindset that I mentioned. It will be a good exercise to write down everything you think is true about money and personal finances. This will help us determine where to help you focus the actions you will need to make for a change."

"OK Miss Chris, you have certainly given us a lot to think about. We are really looking forward to starting this journey and again, we thank you so much! We will see you Friday night!"

"My pleasure." Miss Chris smiled. She always enjoyed starting out with a new couple because she had seen so much growth in a majority the people she and her husband had worked with over the years. She knew that Larry and Sara would be no different.

CHAPTER 3
GETTING READY

Every artist was first an amateur. - *Ralph Waldo Emerson*

Over the next couple of days Larry and Sara started a notebook to keep track of the information Miss Chris had already shared and asked them to gather. They wrote their thoughts, goals, hopes, fears and the comments they heard from others regarding their journey. And just as Miss Chris instructed, they wrote down everything they thought to be true about money.

"Do you think it can be as simple as a mindset and not something in our genes, or where we grew up, or the right type of education? I have always believed that people were either cut out to make a lot of money or they were not, and we just inherited some sort of curse. If it is a mindset, maybe, well..." Larry did not finish his thought. He was afraid to say that even they may be able to change their circumstances. He continued, "have you been keeping track of what Miss Chris asked us to write down, our thoughts about money?"

"I don't really know if it is as simple as a mindset. It seems that we are doing everything we know to do and our friends and family are doing the same. No one we know is really *getting ahead*. Maybe it is our mindset. I have been keeping track, have you been keeping track too? Let's share what we have written. I'll go first," volunteered Sara.

As she opened her notebook, it was obvious that she had written quite a bit and taken this assignment very seriously.

"Wow," remarked Larry, "You really wrote a lot for them."

"Actually, I look at this assignment as one for us, not them. It seems the only thing we say about money is that we do not have enough. We never talk about anything else. I wonder if my parents' perspective is helping or hurting us. I wonder if I have the proper focus. I wonder why they never taught us anything in high school about mutual funds, stocks, bonds, or money markets. I wonder about how we have been programmed and socialized about money and our money choices. I wonder do we have what it takes to be wealthy. I wonder do I limit myself with my fears. I wonder if deep down if I feel a little guilty when we do have a little extra money. I wonder if we have the skills that are needed to make money. When I was at the bank yesterday, the teller asked me if I wanted to open up a CD and I didn't even know what that was. It seems to me, that if we want to have a different financial reality and we have this opportunity, that we should take it very seriously. Have you ever thought about where your money thoughts and perspectives come from?" Sara asked.

"No, I guess I haven't. But I can tell you money is both exciting and scary. I want to make more, but deep down I think that if we do, I will not know what to do with it. I hear about people making good investments, but I don't know what that looks like or how to identify or find a good investment. It seems like I have to listen to two voices, one that tells me I can do it and the other that is constantly reminding me that I can't. I think another part of me tells me that I really don't deserve to be wealthy."

"I feel the same way" Sara agreed.

Larry continued, "When we look at the entire breadth of the financial decisions we have to make, how do we know what to do? For instance, how do we know if we should pay off our house early? How do we know how much life insurance to buy? Should we get term or whole life? How much should we have in our rainy day fund? Should we lease or buy our cars? Should we make the kids pay for some or all of the college education? The questions go on and on. Where do we get the answers? It seems to me that maybe our *programming* is not optimized."

"What do you mean?" asked Sara

"I think we all have been programmed just like computers. We have been taught certain things about money and as a result we react in certain ways. For instance my mom and dad, who grew up in the depression, save everything! They save aluminum foil, reuse nails, keep things forever because they were *programmed* that way. I don't know what our programming is, but I know we have been taught through TV, the media, and today's culture to think and act certain ways about money."

"You are so right! Miss Chris asked us to write down everything we have heard about money, I am adding all that you said to our list."

"You should also add: Money is the root of all evil, the rich get richer and the poor get poorer, money doesn't buy happiness, money doesn't grow on trees, the only way to be rich is to take it from someone else, rich people are greedy and unhappy, you have to work hard to get ahead and have money, not everyone can be rich, you can't be rich and spiritual. Those are all things I have heard about money," Larry added.

After working on this exercise, Larry and Sarah knew they did not currently fall into the wealthy mindset and that they really did not have many positive thoughts about money or really much thought about money except that there was not enough. They studied the characteristics of the wealthy mindset again and decided that they would do what Miss Chris suggested. Take *action*. They would go to Miss Chris' house on Friday and work with this wonderful couple as long as they would work with them, and they would do what it took to become wealthy.

As Friday night approached so did the anticipation and questions. "I wonder if they have a nice home." Larry asked Sara at breakfast on Friday morning.

"I wonder who decorated it or if they have kids," Sara replied back.

"What should we wear?"

Should we bring them a gift?"

Both of them were throwing out questions, but not bothering to answer them. Their minds were really on bigger issues. Larry got Sara's attention by asking, "Should we be 100% honest with them about our financial situation?"

"Yes. I have thought of that and I don't think they can help us if they do not know all the details."

"Do you think they have met others like us? I mean, we are good people, trying to do the right things. But when I think of describing our situation to them, I feel like it will just sound like a country song."

Sara patted his arm. She felt the same way.

As they head out on Friday night their minds, hearts, memories and spirits raced 100 miles per hour. They held hands and prayed they just didn't blow it. All the questions, both spoken and unspoken, filled the car. What if they really were going to learn how to create wealth? Should they allow themselves to hope for something like that? Were they getting their hopes up too high? Was there some kind of magic formula? What if they aren't the right kind of people? What if they don't have the right qualifications or backgrounds? Will they understand what they are about to learn? Will they know what to do with what they learn? How long will it take? Will they have to give up something?

As they found the street, they noticed the other houses in the neighborhood. More questions came. How do people afford these kinds of homes? Do they have maids and gardeners? Could they have a home like this one day? Sara had thought only movie stars lived in houses like this.

They gave themselves a pep talk as they parked in the driveway, they were up to this! They walked up to the door shaking. Was it nerves? Was it fear? Was it excitement? Was it joy?

They knocked on the door and it was opened by a smiling Miss Chris. "Welcome, welcome, thanks for coming!"

"We don't know what to say, your, your, your home is so beautiful." Before Miss Chris could respond, Sara continued "Miss Chris, this is my husband, Larry."

"Very nice to meet you Larry, my husband Lloyd will be down in a moment. He had a phone call he needed to finish up with one of his partners. Why don't we go out on the porch and I'll bring some lemonade."

"You didn't tell me they were *this* rich," whispered Larry to Sara as they followed Miss Chris through the house to the back. They settled themselves into a lovely porch and Miss Chris excused herself to get the pitcher and glasses.

When she returned, they opened the door to help her but she insisted that they sit down and relax.

Relax, easier said than done, thought Larry.

Just then, the door opened and Miss Chris smiled "Oh good Lloyd, this is Sara and Larry."

"It is great to meet you sir," Larry said as he stood and shook Lloyd's hand.

"Sir is a bit formal for my taste, insisted Lloyd, "but you can call me Coach, if that makes you feel more comfortable."

"Oh, so you are a coach? Pro or college, I thought your name sounded familiar."

"I am not *that* kind of coach." Lloyd chuckled. "I would say I am a success coach. I help people go from where they are to where they want to be. I believe that I can shorten your learning curve and put some money in your pockets. So tell me why you are here."

"My wife and I have decided that our life strategy is not working. We seem to be living the life of the baker on the *Duncan Donuts* commercial. We get up, go to work, make the donuts, come home, get up, go to work, and make the donuts.... There has got to more to life than this. When we said 'I do' we both had so many other thoughts and dreams than what we are experiencing. We don't know where we went wrong, but we have decided it is time to find a better way. We realize that if we don't do it now, it will only get worse. We know that soon we will have to pay for the bigger house, then we will be paying for college, and then, then, well by then it may be too late. We are tired of excuses. Today begins a new chapter in our life. We do not believe in coincidences, so the fact that we met your wife and she reached out to Sara and offered us the opportunity to meet with you is the kick in the butt that we needed."

"Great!" exclaimed Coach. "Then let's get right to it. I know Chris shared with you the 4 Pillars or 4P's on the phone, let's start with the first one: **PRINCIPLES.**"

CHAPTER 4

PRINCIPLES

An investment in knowledge pays the best interest. The doorstep to the temple of wisdom is a knowledge of our own ignorance. -- Benjamin Franklin

Coach handed each of them a file folder full of papers. There was also a whiteboard that he moved away from the porch wall. He and Miss Chris had obviously worked with others here at their home before.

"I know that Chris also covered mindsets with you on the phone. I want to remind you of the characteristics of the wealthy mindset:"

- o OPTIMISTIC
- o RISK TAKERS
- o INVESTORS

- DREAMERS | VISIONARIES
- INNOVATIVE
- DECISIVE | COMMITTED

"I want this to be interactive, but there is a lot of material to go over so let's get started. I reminded you of the wealthy mindset and I wanted you to write those at the top of your notebook, because these characteristics are going to be true about you as you work with us. Chris and I believe that there are **4 Pillars of Financial Success** and when you create these pillars and live under them, you will develop in yourselves the mindset of the wealthy. We call these pillars the 4Ps. And the first '**P**' we will go over is **Principles**. A Principle is defined as a fundamental truth, law, or doctrine. There are principles that govern the financial world just as there are those that govern the physical one. Regardless of whether you know what they are, they are operating. Let me give you an example. For centuries the principle of gravity existed but was not defined by man. Regardless of this fact, even if a man did not know the definition of gravity, if he jumped off of a castle, he would have still fallen, right?"

Sara and Larry both nodded. They had been over this one on the phone with Miss Chris.

Coach continued, "There are also general principles of finance that we will share. These principles are ones that Chris and I have discovered along our own journey that we hope you will learn, understand and define. Why don't we do that over our meal."

Coach stood and led them into the dining room as he continued, "The first principle that Chris and I share with the people that we meet is:

Principle: There are rules and you need to learn them

Albert Einstein said, 'You have to learn the rules of the game. And then you have to play better than anyone else.' Have you ever played a game with someone who knew the rules better than you and you thought that they were cheating?"

"Oh sure, I was paying Scrabble last week with my brother, who put up a word that I didn't know and of course, I thought he was cheating." Larry agreed.

"We see many people playing the game of life and money as hard as they can but not getting where they want to go. That tells us, that people don't know the rules, they are playing by old rules, or they aren't very good at the game. The statistics are staggering for the number of people who work their entire lifetime and then have to continue working well into their 70s. They just don't know the rules."

"Is there a rule book for the rich and another for the rest of us?" Larry asked.

"No." replied Coach, "unfortunately, most of these lessons are taught in the school of hard knocks."

"If one of the principles is to understand there are rules and we need to learn them, then why don't we learn about them in school like we do about gravity and civics? I don't remember ever learning about financial principles in school. Did I miss the class?" Larry asked.

Coach smiled gently. "No, you did not miss the class. Unfortunately, the school system does not do a very good job educating people about money in general and in my opinion does a terrible job in teaching people how to make it. I do not know why that is, but it is something that I would love to fix if I could. The financial classroom is the school of hard knocks and for you and Sara, it begins here in our home."

"No one is born fully equipped with the knowledge, skills, attitudes, and values required to live a rich and rewarding life, we must seek these attitudes through continual learning, which is obviously why you and Sara are here." Miss Chris interjected. "This is a great lead-in to our next principle." Miss Chris explained.

Principle: Become a lifelong learner and observer

Miss Chris explained. "Initially, we asked you to understand the principle that there are rules and you need to learn them. Most people feel like they know and follow the rules, yet end up not winning the game. So the next thing you need to learn about financial rules is that they change. Let me give you a couple of historical examples. In the time before the railroad, if you wanted to send a letter, the letter was carried by stage coach or later by the Pony Express. With the advent of the cross continental railroad, it would not have been smart to say, 'I only send letters via stagecoach or Pony Express,' the rules changed. Later, with the advent of the telegraph, letters could be sent over telegraph wires. At that time it would not have been smart to say, 'I only send letters by railroad'. Again, the rules had changed. The rules of financial success are not static, they are very dynamic. It is important to recognize the rules and then develop strategies to maximize your personal gain within the new rules.

"There is a cycle of personal and financial development which begins with the recognition of our strengths and weaknesses and continues with careful examination of the impact of those strengths and weaknesses on all aspects of our lives including our finances. Unfortunately, most people do not take the time to develop in their cycles. You however have decided to continue the process."

"You say continue, but we are just getting started," interrupted Larry.

"Actually, you probably are farther down the path than most. The results and rewards have just not manifested themselves much at this point. It seems to me that you have identified some of your strengths, now we must prioritize goals to address your inefficiencies. Once these goals are established, we must develop the knowledge and skills required to correct the weakest and most problematic areas. Finally, we must honestly assess the outcomes of our efforts, identify residual problems, and repeat the cycle," explained Coach.

"You mean financial success is not a one and done kind of thing?" asked Larry.

"One and done?" Coach and Miss Chris said in unison.

"I always thought there was this one nugget out there somewhere and that if I found it, I would be rich. I never thought of it as a process or what you call a cycle," explained Larry.

"Ah hah," Coach said, "Well, that is one of the perspectives that you currently hold which needs to change. We'll talk more about Perspective as another of the 4 Pillars of Success. For now, I ask you think of your financial life more like an onion rather than a nugget. Once you learn something, you will find another layer to pull back and explore. Once you learn that, you will find another, then another and another. There is an old saying that says, 'formal education will help you make a living, self-education will make you a fortune'. Chris and I educate ourselves, and we will continue to learn as long as we can. This is one of the principles that lead to your financial success. Self-education involves observing, reading, listening, and reflecting. In addition to reading books about successful people and about success principles, most of what we need to learn in life is a result of our ability to observe. We spend a lot of time watching, listening and observing people communicate. We have learned so much about how to communicate with people by observing. Although all of us possess the capacity to observe, highly successful people do it constantly. By reading or studying people, processes, and systems, observant individuals are able to capture what others do and gain insight into why they do and do not do certain things. With practice and consistent use of the information that you and Sara can gather, you will make better decisions and observe what makes some people more successful than others."

Sara piped up, "Let me summarize what you have said so far about the 4 Pillars of Success. The first is Principles. These principles are rules that exist for financial success and it is up to us to learn them by continually learning and observing."

"Excellent summary Sara", Miss Chris encouraged. "We will actually go through a few more principles that Lloyd and I have learned before we call it a night. Let's go back out to the porch to have coffee. Coach can get you started on the next principle we'll cover while I get the coffee ready."

Coach began with the next principle once they were settled back on the porch.

Principle:
There is a price to pay for Financial Success, the price of regret or discipline.

"If you are not already financially independent, or well on your way, you must *choose* to change your behavior and take *action* to get there.

"There are only two paths you can travel once you leave here tonight, the path of discipline or the path of regret. You will either take 100 percent responsibility for changing the financial course of your lives, or you will end up staying with the 95 percent who are headed for financial failure. It is up to you. Only you can decide your future.

"Please do not hide your head under a pillow and pretend things will just somehow work out. They won't. One of the most dangerous attitudes we have seen with the people we know is the *wait and see what happens* attitude. Let me fast forward history for you with that attitude, it is full of regret. You must take action. That is a *reality*. Most people never quite figure out that life is simply a matter of choices. Nothing really forces us to be who we are or where we are in life. We have all made choices that put us exactly where we are at this moment in time. Even bad things that happen in life offer us a choice as to how we will react to them. Bad things happen to all of us. It may be financial. It may be a health challenge. It may be a relationship with your spouse, parents, friends or kids. If you are not happy with where you are or where you are going, you must *choose to change*. It really is that simple. You have probably heard the Chinese proverb, 'The journey of a thousand miles begins with a single step.' It is true. And the first step is choosing. Choose to apply all the lessons you are learning in our time together. See where you may have been operating on the wrong side of the truths and *choose* to do it the right way as you move into the future."

"We like to create acronyms for learning." Miss Chris continued as she served the coffee. "We have created one for this principle: the PARB cycle. Potential leads to Action which leads to Results which leads to Belief, which leads to more Potential which leads to more Action.... "

Coach continued, "You may have heard the term PMA. PMA stands for positive mental attitude. Chris and I used to believe that this was one of the key ingredients of achievement and that if we maintained a positive mental attitude, success was sure to follow. We have come to find out that it is a very important component, and we will discuss this more in the 2nd Pillar of financial success called Perspective; however we now know that positive mental attitude is simply not enough. In fact, we have known people who could crank up such a positive mental attitude they would glow in the dark, but they were still financial failures. We have come to find out that the reason for this was that they simply had not developed the ability to take *action*.

"Attitude without action is worthless. So we have developed an idea where we encourage people to develop a positive mental attitude (PMA) and then we tell them to multiply that by another PMA, Productive Meaningful Action, and that produces PMA^2: Positively Massive Action. Try it. Thomas Henry Huxley once wrote, "The great end of life is not knowledge but action." How true. Knowledge without action is a waste of gray matter. Such knowledge will never benefit a person, or the world around them. Your attitude is critical. The saying, "Attitude determines altitude." Is partially true, you must turn that attitude into action, or it is worthless. And all you have to do is just start. You can always make mid-course corrections. But you cannot correct your course at all if you are not even moving. Take action. And if you really want massive results, take *massive* action!

"The final Principle we will go over helps you understand how to direct the *action* that we just talked about."

Principle:
Creating wealth starts between your ears;
certainty of purpose makes all things possible.

"Life is a series of self-fulfilling prophesies, and they are either positive or negative. Have you wondered why some people are incredibly successful while others with the same or even more apparent skills are not? All humans have potential. Some are able to turn that potential into results that leave us in awe. We believe this is the principle of *certainty of purpose*. Ask yourself what would you try to accomplish if you *knew* that you could not fail? Our lives would look so much different! So often fear holds us all back, simply because we are afraid of failure. To take it one step further, influential people in our life are also afraid of failure so we hear things such as 'Don't get your hopes up'. How many times have we heard this? Whether you are trying to make a team or the choir, your mom said, 'Don't get your hopes up'. When you went on your first date or meet our first true love, we hear, 'don't get your hopes up'. We apply for college or that ideal job and someone tell us, 'don't get your hopes up'. We start a business and we hear our well-meaning friends and family echo the refrain, .."

"Don't get your hopes up", all four of them laughed and said in unison.

"Maybe that is part of the problem we are experiencing as a country right now, our hopes have been minimized. Coach reflected. "I would advise the exact opposite. Get your hopes as high as possible! Be unrealistic! I recognize that mom and dad, friends and family are trying to protect us from a potential crash and fall, but they are inadvertently stealing our dreams as well. If we live our life protecting against hurt, disappointment, and failure, I am not sure that is really living.

"I wonder if Bill Gates had high hopes for Microsoft? I wonder if Steve Jobs was advised to 'not get his hopes up' when he started Apple? I wonder if it was realistic for Mark Zuckerberg of Facebook to be a billionaire in his 20's? I had high hopes when I started out in business. As a matter of fact, it was those high hopes that allowed us to persevere through the tough times. It was those high hopes that allowed us to set bigger and better goals. It was those high hopes that allowed us focus when distractions came our way. It was high hopes that allowed me to court my wife. Without high hopes, I may even be dead."

"Wow, I never thought about it like that. Are you saying that we are *too* realistic?" asked Larry.

"Look around and you will see a lot of people lower their expectations because of their fear of disappointment. This is their life strategy. Conventional wisdom tells them that if they don't expect much, the worst that can happen is that they won't be disappointed, disillusioned or frustrated. When things don't turn out the way that they expect them to work out, the best that can happen is they will be pleasantly surprised if they do work out.

"What if we were to apply this principle to business? There's the so-called 'conventional wisdom' business axiom, Under-promise and over-deliver. If your customer or client does not expect much because you are not trying to sell them the moon, then they can only be satisfied with whatever you deliver, because it was expected. Or, even better, they may be pleasantly surprised because you delivered them more. That seems reasonable, right?"

"Sure." said Larry. "They teach us that at the office. Don't over-promise because we won't be able to deliver. As a matter of fact, we just had meetings with the sales department to make sure that sales and delivery are on the same page."

"We think this is wrong!" Miss Chris said passionately. "When it comes to marketing a product or service, if you under-promise there will not be anybody to deliver that product to! Who would be interested? Think of the marketing, 'What I have to offer is okay'. Marketing should scream 'This product will knock your socks off!' or 'This product will meet and exceed your needs.'

Coach said,"I bet I know what you are thinking. The typical response that we get, more times than we can count, is 'I don't want to promise something I can't deliver.' Who said anything about over-promising? We are not talking about making a big promise. If we do make a big promise, then yes it is a great idea to keep it. The approach is to make sure whatever you promise is something you can indeed deliver, but never under-promise!"

"But don't people understate themselves or their products because they don't want to appear cocky, conceited, or because they want to be realistic?" asked Sara.

"Sure." Coach agreed "but a lot of the time, it is just the usual suspect at play, fear. When people make a big promise, the pressure is on to come up with the goods at the highest level. If there is a big promise out there, it's going to put the pressure on you in a positive way, to be your best. Remember, it is the unrealistic who accomplish the most.

"Today consumers and the marketplace are changing at lightning speed. It doesn't take much for a prospect's attention to go elsewhere. If you do not tell customers why they should buy from you, but your competitors do, then guess who gets the customers? We have to start expecting more from ourselves. We can do more, be more and achieve more, even if we don't have all the answers right now.

"We may have been let down or even let someone down at some point, but it worked ok didn't it? We learned something or we know better now, don't we? We have to

37

believe that it is ok if we fail. This is the principle of *certainty*. Certainty allows us to stretch ourselves and accomplish more because we *know* that we cannot fail."

Larry and Sara smiled as Coach finished up his last point so passionately. Larry commented, "It is interesting that the first principles of financial success you have just shared with us have nothing to do with dollars and cents. Sara and I thought that you were going to tell us to make more, invest in real estate, live on less than we make, or buy this stock or that stock. But what I hear you say is that we need to begin with choosing to change, take action, stay away from fear, don't be too realistic and commit to learning. These are all things even I can handle!"

"I'm excited to hear you say that. I am also excited for you both; you are already on your way to financial success!" Miss Chris cheered.

"I know it is getting late, but can you hang on for a few more lessons for tonight?" Coach asked.

"Yes!" Larry and Sara both said enthusiastically. They were absorbed with what Coach and Miss Chris had been sharing with them and they had not even considered the time.

"We began with stating that there are financial rules and you need to continually learn them. We will now share a few more important rules that you can think about before our next meeting. We want you to leave tonight with the sense that some of the old safe rules are the new *risky*.

"Pull out that first sheet of paper in your folder. I am a visual learner so I want to show you this. This is a tool that we have used for a number of years to illustrate how people can live their lives, the next Principle:"

Principle: Live in Significance

"This is what we call CS Triangle. We have developed this little triangle to help people visualize one of the aspects of life- we call it the Crisis/ Survival/ Success/ Significance triangle- CS for short."

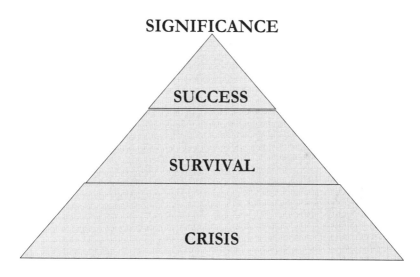

"Most people live here," Coach pointed to the line between Crisis and Survival. "They have a crisis, solve it, start surviving and then fall right back in to a crisis. Let me give you a quick example. Let's take the average family, they are getting by and the washer breaks down...CRISIS! They figure out how to solve that, and start surviving and boom, the furnace breaks down...CRISIS! They solve it and boom, something else happens. Up and down they go from crisis to survival and back again. Back and forth, back and forth, they go, forever.

"There are others that live above that on this line", he pointed to the line between Survival and Success. "Less people live here, but a lot of Americans still do. An example of life on this line would be something like this. A businessman closes a deal and he is successful, he loses a client, back to survival. He hires a great employee, he is feeling successful, the tax bill comes and he is back to survival. Back and forth, back and forth, they go.

"A lesson I learned decades ago and I still remember vividly, if you combine the CS Triangle with the right mindset, which has such a crucial importance in life especially in one's 'financial mindset', you can truly live here." Coach pointed to the word Significance at the top of the triangle.

"There is a small group of Americans that live in the world between Success and Significance. Most people think that nothing bad ever happens to those that live here. Not true! As a matter of fact, they may even have more 'bad' things happen to them, but the key is their mindset. Things that happen do not become a crisis. They are not categorized as problems; they are simply issues that need to be solved. So the big question for you, my young friends is this, what is the difference?"

"I used to think the rich just get richer and now I still believe that, but..." replied Larry.

Sara finished his sentence. "The rich do get richer but there are some specific reasons why this happens and we have a new notebook full of principles and rules that are going to help us get there!"

Coach and Miss Chris both smiled. This couple was going to be fun to work with; they were catching on so quickly. "That's right. We have a few more principles to cover. The next one is:

Principle:
Employment has changed; create other means of revenue.

"What was once true in terms of employment is no longer true. In your parents generation it was unusual for someone to work for more than one employer in their lifetime, let alone work for more than one employer at the same time.

"Let's look at the numbers. The second sheet in the folder is an accumulation of some research that we have done about the system *they* teach and the reality of the results.

"Who is the *they* that you are referring to?" Larry asked as he looked over the paper.

"You know, the infamous *they* that tell us how and why to do things and yet nobody I have ever met knows them. *They* have the idea you should go to college, get good grades, get a good job and you will retire and live happily ever after."

"Oh Yes, I have not only heard that, but I guess I have been following *them*," Larry agreed.

"Lets look at the research we have come up with. As you can see, it is an age profile and the median net worth of that age group. My guess is the people that you work with and most of the people you associate are *below* the net worth median for their age group. In our experience the only way to get *above* the net worth median is to own your own business or assets. We'll discuss this more, but let's look at the numbers.

Age[5]	Average Income	Median Income
Under 35	$106,000	$11,800
35 to 44	$325,600	$86,600
45 to 54	$661,200	$182,500
55 to 64	$935,800	$253,700
65 to 74	$1,015,200	$239,400
75 over	$638,200	$213,500

Age Profile[6]	% of Pop.	Median Net Worth
Under 25	15.99 %	$9,660
25-29	29.35 %	$37,229
30-34	20.76 %	$136,629
35-39	14.58 %	$298,500
40-44	7.63 %	$491,100
45-49	3.65 %	$690,090
50-54	1.89 %	$702,552
55-59	1.12 %	$1,123,000
60-64	0.38 %	$507,000
65 and over	12.99 %	$2,294,492

Mean Income Statistics

- Working for someone else: $350,100

- Retired: $543,100

- Self-employed: $1,961,300

"Today, it is highly unusual for someone to work for one employer their entire life. We believe and actually know of lots of people that believe you should have multiple things going on at the same time."

"That's right Chris." Coach agreed. We have more to say about that, when we talk about another of the 4 Pillars, **Practice**.

"We have really gone over quite a bit of information tonight. I am sure that we are breaking through some of the rules and mindsets that you have always believed. But look at the time!", exclaimed Miss Chris. "I am going to have to call it a night. You too Lloyd, we have an early appointment tomorrow, so it looks like we will have to have you guys back to continue our discussions. Next week? Same time, same place?"

"We wouldn't miss it for the world." Larry and Sara said enthusiastically. They both smiled warmly at each other. They had not agreed with each this often about so much, for a very long time. They were excited to be on this adventure together.

"We enjoy this topic so much, and love to share with other couples. We will look forward to meeting with you again, but let me leave you with this final principle. I promise Chris, it will not take long."

Principle: Create some of your own Rules

"One of the books I read recently was Maria Shriver's *Ten Things I Wish I Had Known before Going into the Real World*. It had some great points. We have borrowed a couple of her points and have come up with a couple of our own and these are principles and rules that we currently live by. We suggest that you work together and circle some of your own as well.

"A couple of hers that we like are:

- Marriage is work
- Be willing to fail
- Your behavior has consequences
- Don't expect anyone to support you financially
- Laughter needs to be a daily behavior

"We have added five more of our own:

- Life is not fair
- People will let you down
- Life is not linear, sometimes you have to go backwards in order to go forward
- There is a difference between being financially ambitious and financially hopeful
- If everyone is going right, it is probably better to go left

"And now, my new friends, I believe it is best if we call it a night."

They all stood as Larry and Sara gathered up their things and headed to the door.

"Thank you again Coach, Miss Chris. We are so appreciative of your time and for working with us." Sara said as she hugged them.

"You have given us a lot to think about." Larry added before leading Sara to their car.

QUESTIONS TO PONDER AND ACTIONS TO TAKE

Do you agree that the rich get richer?

What do you believe about the rules outlined in this chapter?

If the rich know rules or principles that you do not, how do you plan to narrow that knowledge gap?

Do you know anyone like Larry and Sara? Are you?

Fast forward your life. If you stay on the path that you are on and continue to do what you are doing, will you have the life that you desire? If not, what are you willing to do to change it?

Do you have a mentor in your life? Is there someone that could be a mentor if you asked them?

Make a list of things you would like to buy or do if you were not living in your present financial situation. Some have even made a *dream board* full of pictures of places that they would like to visit, cars they would like to drive, houses that they would like to have, etc.

Read, read, and read. There are hundreds if not thousands of "financial help books".

Find a local seminar on financial basics. (Kiyosaki, Ecker, Bach)

CHAPTER 5
PERSPECTIVES

Now looking back I realize...How hard it is to recognize...Opportunity in disguise. -- Lari White/Craig Wiseman/David Kent, Stepping Stone

The next Friday could not come fast enough for Larry and Sara. They had gone over their notes throughout the week, took inventory of their assets and income and reflected upon what they learned. They were beginning to believe that financial success could be in their future.

Miss Chris once again greeted them at the door and led them out to the porch. Lloyd was there enjoying a book and the beautiful evening. The table was beautifully set up with dinner ready.

"Ah, our new friends return. So we haven't scared you off?"

"Absolutely not!" replied Larry as they shook hands. "In fact just the opposite, we were so excited to come and learn more from both of you. Were you kidding around with us or have you really scared people off?"

"Let me ask the question another way" Sara jumped in. "I have been wondering something since I first met Miss Chris at the coffee shop. How many couples do you work with? I mean with all the information and hope that you have shared with us, it seems to me that there would be a waiting list just to get invited to your home."

Coach chuckled softly and replied "not as many as you would think. We have asked ourselves that question so many times over the years. What if we opened a little office for financial counseling? Would we have any clients? Our conclusion is that we would have a lot of tire kickers, but very few that stick with it. It takes commitment and discipline to do more than talk about having a better life and getting to the next level."

Miss Chris ushered everyone to the table and began to serve. Larry and Sara settled in with their notebooks close by.

Coach began, "Tonight we are going to cover the second pillar of financial success: What we like to refer to as **Perspective**. Webster defines Perspective as: a way or manner of looking at life and life's events."

"Chris and I believe everyone should take a look at the fruit of their lives, the results. When they do take at look at the fruit of their lives, maybe they don't like it, maybe it doesn't taste so good, maybe the results are small or there aren't any results or not enough results. Regardless, this strange fruit did not just come out of nowhere. You have to be able to ask the hard questions and sometimes the answer to these questions can be a little uncomfortable or even painful."

"What questions?" Larry inquired.

"Questions about the perspectives you have about yourself and your life. Who are you? How do you think? What are your beliefs? What are your habits? What are your traits? How do you *really* feel about yourself? How confident are you in yourself? How confident are you in others? Are you able to take action in spite of fear and worry? Are you able to take action in spite of inconvenience, discomfort or when you are not in the right mood?"

Miss Chris continued thoughtfully, "You have been open with us and have described your current financial situation and work life. You have come to realize that things are the way they are, so now the questions come. You have already starting asking yourself some important questions. Can the situation be changed? Do we work for others, ourselves or not at all? Do we earn a lot of money, a little money or a moderate amount of money? Where do we put our money if we have extra? Are we savers or spenders? Are we risk takers? Do we love what we do? The answer to these questions will expose the perspectives you have of yourselves. That is our goal for tonight's meeting, to help you understand your current perspectives and identify if you would like, or are willing, to change them. It can be uncomfortable."

"So we are going to cover those question's tonight?" Sara asked.

"Not entirely." Miss Chris responded. "We are going to ask you to examine the results of your life and your way of being. We will ask you to look at your life and *this* will tell you what you *must* believe for these results to be present."

You control how you see the world

"The truth is our lives are the way they are because of what we can control, not because of circumstances we cannot control. Although people do not always take the time to do so, we do have control of our belief system. We always act or do not act in accordance with our beliefs."

"That's right" Coach began. "Chris and I believe that you can control how you see the world, that you can control your perspective."

"Before we get started, I do have another question. You touched on it when you showed us CS thought last week. How do you stay living in Significance? Are there always ups and downs, or do you reach a point in your life that life is not a struggle?" Larry inquired.

Coach replied, "That is a good question and the answer lies in your perspective. There are always going to be issues because life is bigger than any of us individually. None of us control the economy. We have had severe economic recessions, actually we have had 8 since 1960, and we will probably have a few more. We have had whole world economies change before. Social and political controversy is nothing new. Yet, as wildly as the pendulum swings, the world always seems to move back through stages of equilibrium. No matter how bad things may seem, there will be an upswing at some point. Just because we cannot see it, does not mean we should not be preparing for it. This is not mere positive thinking. We believe that most people are not preparing for eventual success and happiness, they seem to have given up on themselves and the success that they can have. We like to ask those people, what the heck are you doing? The very sad fact is, most people don't reach their full potential, even when the economy is booming, because most people operate on a very basic level of life based only on what they believe to be true and they are not willing to look deeper. That is another reason is why we love to meet with couples in a setting like this."

Miss Chris continued, "We hope to encourage you to be who or what you strive to be now! We expect you to show up in excellence even when you think there is really nothing on the line. The truth is, there is always something on the line, *you*! Your principles. Your perspectives. Your lifestyle. Your kids' future. Your actions. Your results. We constantly have to till our own soil no matter what. Only then will we be in a position to reap the rewards of the inevitable change of seasons."

Coach nodded and added, "Absolutely no one can overestimate the power of the mind and its role in our success! It is imperative to keep our minds right and on the right track if we are to achieve balanced success in our finances as well as the other areas of our lives such as health, emotions, relationships and spiritual practices.

"The analogy we like to use for the 2nd Pillar of Success, Perspective, is a radio station."

Choose to Tune In

"Suppose there was a *Success* station. The only way you can hear a radio station is to be tuned into it. If you are just slightly off the right station, you cannot get the full affect. All of us grow up listening to some sort of radio, the question is, which station? Perhaps you grew listening to YCDT (You Can't Do That). When you tried to ride your bike you were told YCDT. When you tried to make the varsity team you were told YCDT. When you wanted to go to college, get a nice car, start a business, you were told YCDT. Well that radio program needs to change, so it is up to us to change the station."

Miss Chris continued, "Maybe you grew up YCHT (You can't have that). When you wanted your first bike or Barbie you were told YCHT or maybe it was WCAT (We can't afford that). When you wanted a new outfit you were told YCHT or WCAT. Maybe it was an XBox, computer, iPod, cell phone you wanted when you heard WCAT. Coach and I want to encourage you to *change the station.*"

"That's right." Coach started. "The station you tune into is your choice. No one can force you listen to a particular station. If you do not like what is playing, *change the station*."

"We live in a world today where we are bombarded with messages. Experts tell us most of these messages are negative. It's not easy to find the positive stations but they are out there, so if you are listening to negative one…"

"*Change the station!*" Larry and Sara chimed in. Larry then asked "but what station should we listen to?"

"Good question." Coach responded. "You should listen to YCAM (You can achieve more). The radio station can be compared to our own mind and beliefs about success. If our minds and our thoughts get sidetracked, our success will get sidetracked. If the station is not clear you will hear static and that is very annoying. As we learn to keep our minds tuned into YCAM, our bodies will then carry out our success and we will begin to experience abundance!"

Miss Chris continued, "We understand that all you have to do is turn on the news and there are plenty of reasons not to be optimistic about a lot of things. Sometimes I wonder if the whole media experience is designed to discourage, disappoint and disengage us. To us, the most important part of the life experience is to recognize that we have the choice of how we are going to perceive ourselves within this process. There's an old saying about being in the right place at the right time. I think it is missing an important component. I am convinced that it is not enough to be in the right place at the right time. You have to be the right *person* in the right place at the right time. If you are not the 'right' person you may not even recognize that it is the right place at the right time."

Choose the Positive

Coach explained, "One of my favorite authors, Charles Dickens, wrote in 1859, 'It was the best of times, it was the worst of times, it was the age of wisdom, it was the age of foolishness, it was the epoch of belief, it was the epoch of incredulity, it was the season of Light, it was the season of Darkness, it was the spring of hope, it was the winter of despair, we had everything before us, we had nothing before us, we were all going direct to heaven, we were all doing direct the other way'.

"One of the most important perspectives about money is to incorporate a positive focus while also understanding that we live in a universe of duality as Dickens so eloquently put it. We have good/bad, up/down, light/dark, black/white, right/left, in/out. You cannot have a back without a front. This duality is always going to exist, no matter what. It existed for Dickens 150 years ago, and will exist 150 years from now. You are not going to have upside in your life without a downside, and vice-versa. So what do we do? It is our choice. If you always see the negative side of things because that is what you choose to look at, then all that exists for you at that time will be, what?"

"The downside," Larry finished, "as a matter of fact, we have some friends like that. No matter what, it is bad. They are going on vacation and they fret about packing. They get home and they fret about work. They fret about their kids, their money. It is very tough to spend time with them because we always leave feeling deflated and depressed."

"Exactly." Miss Chris agreed. "However, if you choose to see the positive side, what will exist for you? The positive. You and I know none of this is new, but how many people actually live this way? We get sucked into other mindsets and we get into a habit of seeing things on the negative side and we think that that is what is. To me that is the hilarious part. We think that what we see is reality. No! It is your reality! Your perspective just made it your reality. Life happens to all of us. It is our perspective about what happens that makes it a positive or negative. It is up to us what we will do with what happens in life and what it will become. I don't know anyone who has not had something bad happen to them. It could have been a health issue, a financial issue, a relationship issue; the ultimate question is not how to avoid bad things, because that is impossible, the question is how will you handle it?"

"Now let's get something straight. Chris and I are not gurus sitting on some mountain somewhere with no negative thoughts ever crossing our mind. We know that is impossible. Everyone has negative thoughts. The difference is we choose not to let that stuff live inside us. Bad things and negative thoughts are going to happen. The question is how long will you stay stuck in them? We have learned what determines how long you stay stuck is,"

"Your perspective!" Miss Chris filled in.

"Yes, that is all it is. Change your habit by practicing positive focus. You practice and you move on."

Challenge your beliefs

"Let's touch on some of the other radio stations we have heard growing up. One of the issues that most of us face is the negative programming that we receive from a very young age. 'You can't do that', 'you can't be that', 'watch out for rich people they always have an angle'. The list is endless and the impact is far-reaching. The end result is that when you start to recognize the negative programming and start to find ways to reprogram, you can create a state in your mind called mixed messaging."

"Mixed messaging? I am not familiar with that terminology, said Larry.

"Let me explain it this way," Coach continued. "All of us have *file folders* in our minds. These folders help us keep track of events, emotions, history, and just about everything we think and feel. As we continue to gather experiences and information through life, sometimes those file folders start to have conflicting data in them. For instance, maybe your pastor preaches a message about the abundant life of God, but you look at your checkbook and there is not abundance there. These incidents in our lives are what we call mixed messages. Mixed messages create mixed results. Another example, if you want to start your own business but believe that you do not have the experience, you will act accordingly and never have the experience of starting your own business. If you believe that you do not have enough money to manage, you will not manage your money, which will result in you never having enough money to manage."

"We must periodically challenge our own perspectives and beliefs. If we don't, it is like driving with your foot on the gas pedal and on the brake at the same time. We may say and believe we want to get to somewhere, yet some of our beliefs hold us back. We have got to revise some of the *file folders* of our mind and add some new ones. This allows us to make new choices. We want to add perspectives that support happiness and success versus those that do not. We want to delete the old or misappropriate perspectives, or at least neutralize them. There is a psychological concept called cognitive dissonance, have you heard the term?"

Larry and Sara looked at each other blankly, and admitted that, "No we have never heard that term."

"We all have beliefs and most people act in accordance with those beliefs. Psychologists tell us when we do not act in accordance with our beliefs it creates all kinds of psychological imbalances which they call cognitive dissonance. We like to think that we derive our beliefs based on rational decisions or the facts. That is partly true, but the whole truth is that we still mostly act on what we believe rather than facts. How long ago was it that people believed the sun revolved around the earth or that the earth was flat? Because we mostly act on what we believe, it is important to choose what we believe."

Choose to learn from your mistakes and move forward

"Let me tell you a story about perspective. When I was a young boy, my father taught me how to ride a bike. At first, he held onto the back of my seat and ran with me. Then, as time went on, he started to let go. Right before I would fall, he would grab the bike to steady me. Then one day, he just let me fall. Crying, I asked, 'Why didn't you catch me?' My dad replied, 'If I didn't let you fall, you would never learn how to stay up. Once you learn to identify what it feels like when you are beginning to fall, you will be able to learn how to make the proper corrections not to fall.' At the time I did not understand that my Father was teaching me a very valuable lesson."

"What a great lesson. We covered mistakes and failure as part of the success principles and mindsets last week; wealth begins between the ears. So it is not only a Principle, it is also a Perspective?" Larry asked.

"That's right. Our perspective of the mistakes or failures that we have made can make all the difference in how we live. Let me ask you a question, what are you afraid of?" questioned Coach.

"I guess that I have to say failure", confessed Larry

"I thought you might say that." said Coach. "We have come to understand that failure is really the first part of the success cycle. I used to avoid situations that I couldn't control because I might fail. I used to avoid uncomfortable situations because I might fail. I used to avoid meeting new people because I might fail. At that time my life was about avoidance of failure *not* about growing toward success. Life is different now. I recognize now that failure is just the first step in the success cycle. If you do not fail, you do not have the opportunity to grow or succeed."

"How do you develop that perspective in life?" Larry wondered.

Coach responded, "Our belief is that you must be prepared for a surprise and the surprise might be a negative surprise.

Expect Surprises

Something is going to happen in your day, whether you are late because you got stuck behind a train or your car had a flat tire, something is going to happen. The key is your ability not to take mole hills and look at them as mountains. Problems are a normal part of life and change. Things are changing so rapidly that there are going to be problems you face. So you must look at failure as an event, not as a person. I am not a failure. Maybe I have had a failure or a temporary inconvenience. Maybe I have had a stumbling block, but the idea is to turn the stumbling block into a steppingstone, and step on it instead of stumbling over it. Look at failure as the fertilizer of success. Fertilizer stinks, it smells. You see that guy putting it on his lawn and you say, 'Wow, that guy is fertilizing his lawn.' Do the same when you fertilize your mistakes. Don't wallow in them, lay in them or roll in them. Pick yourself up off your mistakes and learn from them and try not to repeat that same thing again. Look at it as a temporary inconvenience, as a detour, not as a failure. I try to avoid the 3Ws at all times- Wallowing, Whining, and Waiting."

"I have never thought of it that way. I have had a lot of what I thought of 'failures'. In reality they are lessons for the things that work and things that don't. Perhaps I have taken them too personally or made them into mountains." Sara exclaimed.

"We have all either seen, experienced or heard of someone who made the proverbial mountain out of a molehill. The consequences can vary anywhere from entertaining, to frustrating to even tragic. The everyday tragedy though, is that so many people continue to assess a negative perspective on life's circumstances when they could just as easily do the opposite." Miss Chris agreed.

"You are right Miss Chris," Sara interjected, "I was talking with a girlfriend recently and she was really upset about something her son had done. She went on and on about this incident. All I could think was that it was such a small incident, eventually you won't even remember it."

"That is a great example of observing and perspective." Coach complimented. "But let me point out, it is *your* perspective that your friend is making the proverbial mountain out of a molehill. Maybe this is your perspective because your son did the same thing and you found out, over time, that it is not something to be upset about. Perhaps, it is simply a matter of maturity or it was never that big a deal to you. Regardless, it is your opinion that what your friend is going through is a small incident, it is obviously her belief that it is a large incident."

Beliefs are strong opinions

Miss Chris removed the dinner plates as she continued the conversation. "What we hope you are beginning to see is that perspectives and your beliefs are at best only strong opinions. Beliefs color and filter our view of everything. They create our perspectives. The problem is, we get used to these filters and forget that we have them on, then we believe that the way we see things is the way things are, which of course may not always be the case. Whether you are naturally a pessimistic or just facing uncertainty due to the current economic climate, our hope is that you will develop the skill of challenging your negative, unconscious beliefs."

Let's not agree

"Here is a fun game." Coach continued, "Join in just about any random conversation and ask the question, 'Can you believe some of the things people think these days?'

You will most likely find someone who would not agree with you. There is always a reason for us to think some other people are crazy just because we all have our particular world view. I have found that when someone gets a little more specific about their beliefs, things change. For instance, someone may say to you 'I can't believe people think XYZ'. Some people might agree with them, some might give them a horrified look and respond, 'Well, actually, I can't believe people think ZYX!' Then you are either in for a lively debate or some seriously awkward moments. In the end, our beliefs are neither true nor false; they can only be supportive or not supportive of our success and happiness. They can be empowering or prohibitive."

Be flexible

"It has been our observation that sometimes our beliefs get so iron-clad into our nervous system that they turn into inflexible conclusions about life. Especially if the beliefs were unconsciously and often accidentally imprinted into us as children when we have far less experience to really draw educated distinctions between a temporary situation and something that seems permanent and irreversible. This causes two problems. The first is that those people get label as opinionated and force people out of their lives. The second problem is that most people never re-examine the map of life that they drew when they were children, or seek to revise it to reflect upon whom they are today and who they want to be tomorrow." Coach stated.

"Eventually, we move away from belief into full *knowing*, the knowing that comes from believing in something more than what may be evident on the surface, and the wisdom that comes from the experience of testing those beliefs in *the real world*."

"Another piece of advice on this topic of beliefs or perspective is that you need to be careful what you believe. It can do more than start a heated argument; it can stop you in your tracks before you have even gotten started on your journey."

Perspective colors what we believe

"Let's look at some pictures to show you examples of how our perspective colors or filters what we think to be true."

Coach pulled out a picture from his folder. "What do you see, an old hag or pretty young lady?"

"I see an old lady, where is the young girl?" Sara offered.

"I see the young lady, but no old lady," replied Larry.

"Interesting" said Coach. "Perspectives are fascinating aren't they? Are you sure that that is what you see?"

"Sure," said Sara with a tint of doubt.

"Just because you see it one way and Larry sees it another does not make one of you wrong and one right. Sometimes there is no right or wrong, there is only different."

"What do you see here?" Coach asked as he showed them the next picture.

"I see a vase," Sara said.

"I see two faces." exclaimed Larry.

"Once again, you are both right. The point in looking at these pictures is to help you see that if you start with the assumption that one person has to be right and one person has to be wrong, there is little ability to connect, and this leads to miss-communication," explained Coach.

"How so?" asked Sara.

"Have you ever had a conversation and you thought you were on the same page only to find out later that you weren't? One of the big reasons this happens is perspective. You could be using words that you both understand but have no understanding at all."

"This could explain the time when Larry told me he would be home in a little bit and I interpreted it as minutes and he meant hours. I was so mad at him!"

"Exactly," Coach responded. "The reality is that you thought you were on the same page and you weren't even in the same book. This happens because of different perspectives. You perceive a word or phrase or thought one way and the other person perceives it differently. I want to emphasize again, there is no right and no wrong, it is just different."

"Okay, one more picture. What do you see this time?"

"A musician!" shouted Sara.

"I see a woman's face but I can also see the saxophone player," Larry added.

"It is our backgrounds and experiences that determine how we perceive things. Here are three relatively simple examples and you discovered firsthand how you perceived things differently."

Perspective of Money

"Now, let's apply those thoughts to money. Larry, do you know how to get rich?" Coach asked.

"By making more money?" Larry responded with hesitation.

"What do you perceive more or a lot of money to be?"

"Well, certainly a lot more than we have."

"Is there a number you can attach to *more* or *a lot*?" questioned Coach.

"I never thought about that," replied Larry.

"Let me ask Sara the same question. What do you perceive *a lot* of money to be?" repeated Coach.

"To me, a lot of money depends on the context. For instance, if I am shopping and am looking to buy a product and one brand is $2.00 more than another, then $2.00 is a lot of money. If we are looking to stay at a hotel for a vacation and I find two rooms and one is $100 a night and the other is $200 per night, $100 is a lot of money. If we are talking about a lot of money for a decision we need to make about buying something, then I would say $1000.00 is a lot. Another way that I look at it is, if Larry came home and said he spent $50.00 on something, I would be ok with that. But if he came in and said that he spent $500 on something, we would definitely have words."

"A very wise response Sara; Have you guys ever had this discussion before?" Miss Chris asked.

"No, the depths of our money discussions have been how to make more or not spend as much. We had no idea how to accomplish this and we did not have any idea that our own perspectives impacted the issues. It seems that everything we have tried. We end up taking one step forward but two steps backwards. It is pretty discouraging to be brutally honest with you," Sara explained, dejected.

"May I share an experience with you two?" Larry asked.

"Sure, it seems we have been doing a lot of the talking. I'd like to hear from you," Coach agreed.

"The other day Sara and I and were out with some friends and the subject of money came up, specifically how to make more of it. One of our friends made a comment that he had all the money that he would ever need. I looked at him to check to see if he was joking and I could tell that he was very serious about his comment. I know where he lives, what he drives, where he vacations. I know he doesn't have his own jet or vacation home. How does somebody believe that they have all the money they need when they don't have much more than we do?"

No limits

"What a great observation and question!" Miss Chris encouraged. "Obviously, I don't know your friend, but unfortunately there are quite a few individuals that have this same belief and they live their lives as your friend does. In my experience, they do this for a couple of possible reasons. The first is that they have given up on their dreams of a better life and have come to accept the status quo. Maybe they set some goals years ago and they got squashed. Maybe they experienced some ridicule, like you did when you spoke to your associates at work. Maybe they had high hopes and life got in the way. I have met hundreds of people like this. The interesting thing is if you talk to kids 5-7 years old, *all* of them have big dreams. They want to be astronauts and professional ball players and doctors, all at the same time! Society gradually lets them know what they can and cannot do and veils it in the form of being *realistic*."

"The big reason is that they have given up on themselves and convince themselves that they aren't good enough for the better things in life. They convince themselves they are where they are and that is all that it is going to be. They have the perspective that they have reached the limit. The truth is there is no limit," Coach added.

"I like to use an example in history when we talk about limits and breaking them. Do you know the story about the 4 minute mile?"

"I used to run on the high school team so I know that Roger Bannister was the first to break the 4 minute mile, but how does that relate to money?" questioned Larry.

"Since the beginning of time people held the belief that is was impossible for a human being to run the mile less than 4 minutes. However in 1954, Bannister did the impossible. He achieved this not merely by physical practice but by constantly rehearsing the event in his mind. In his mind he would break through the 4 minute barrier so many times with so much emotional intensity that he created vivid references that became an unquestioned command to his body to produce the desired result. Many people don't realize that the greatest aspect of his breakthrough was what it did for others. It had once seemed that no one would ever break the 4 minute mile, yet within one year of Bannister's achievement, 37 other runners also broke it."

"Perspective seems to be very important in financial success. Are you saying that we are *thinking* wrong, because all these years we thought we were *doing* something wrong." Sara asked.

"That is why Perspective is one of the 4 Pillars. Are you familiar with the story of the two shoe salesman?" Coach inquired.

"The story with the two salesmen who get shipwrecked and end up on a deserted island and they notice no one wears shoes. One salesman suggested that they won't be able to sell anything, but the other looks and says that they will make a fortune." Larry blurted out.

"That's the one," Coach replied happily. "Opportunities exist for everyone, even you, if you have the correct perspective."

"Let me tell you about another one." Coach went on. "In March 1991 it was reported in *Forbes* magazine that two new cars, the Mitsubishi Eclipse and the Chrysler-Plymouth Laser had entered the market. The Chrysler dealers were averaging about 13 sales per dealership. Mitsubishi, on the other hand, averaged over 100! You may say, 'what else is new?' The Japanese were beating us soundly then. The unique thing about these two cars is that they were exactly the same; they were built in partnership between the two companies. The only difference is the name and the nameplate. How could this be, you may ask? The research has shown that people want to buy Japanese cars because they perceive them to be better quality. The problem in this case, and many others, it is a false perspective. The American car was the same quality because it was the very same car. Another interesting fact about this story is that Japanese products have gone from nonexistent, to be considered junk, to be premium products and now back to having quality issues, and that has been in my lifetime."

"I always thought that the rich were different, you know kind of lucky. They seem to be in the right place at the right time and fate smiled on them. Now I understand that is not all there is to it. Our perspective was off. You make it sound like all we need to do is have a positive perspective and that our money problems will go away. Can it really be that easy?" Larry wondered out loud.

"There are actually a number of perspectives that hold people down and the one you just mentioned is a big one." Coach replied. "There are others we will discuss and that you will discover on your own. Remember perspective is the way one looks at life and life's events.

"One of my favorite books is '*As a Man Thinketh*' by James Allen. He wrote 'good thoughts and actions can never produce bad results; bad thoughts and actions can never produce good results'. When I was a young boy my family grew tomatoes. We grew tomatoes by planting tomatoes. We didn't grow them by planting anything else. It works the same way in the mental and moral world, you reap what you sow; you cannot reap what you have not sown. If you want good and positive results, you have to sow good and positive thoughts in yourself and others. It is amazing that people see it easily in the natural world but not the mental world. It is not as obvious that the quality of people's thinking leads to the quality of their results. One of the reasons most people do not reach their dreams is that they desire to change their results without changing their perspectives.

Expectation management

"One final thought as it relates to perspective, *expectation management*. What do you expect financially? It has been our experience that if you expect to have no money at the end of the month, you won't. If you expect to have some, you will. You have to learn to set your expectations higher. We have seen that most people are broke because being broke is what they expect. Let me share a story of a couple we worked with a few years ago. This couple had been married for about 25 years. They had a couple of kids and *never* had any money. They had made a decision that mom would work and dad would stay home and watch the kids. We asked them where all their money went. They told us that it all went to pay the bills. As we peeled back the onion, which always brings tears, we were astonished."

"Astonished?" Larry questioned.

"Yes. And here's why. When we asked to walk through where the money went, we recognized that little, wrong decisions can have a big impact. We asked them if they had

72

a budget. No, they responded, they did not have any money so why spend the time budgeting for zero. As we walked through the money, we were more and more disturbed and began to realize why a recent survey has indicated that almost 80% of Americans live paycheck to paycheck. As I recall they were making about $60,000 per year. Keep in mind that this is for a family of four and they have *no* money left over at the end of the month, ever."

"Let me show you on paper." Coach opened his notebook to draw it out for them.

"Let's walk through the numbers. As you can see, they are making about $5k per month, after taxes they are bring home about $3700. I asked them how much they paid for their house payment. They didn't have a mortgage because they have rented for 25 years. When I asked why, their response was that they could never save up the down payment. After rent and utilities, they had about $3000. Their car note is $128. I thought that didn't sound bad, until they told me that was a weekly amount, another poor decision. That leaves them with $2400+. They paid about $400 per month for rental and car insurance. We learned they have never shopped around for lower rates, another bad decision. Still after this, they have $2000 a month. Then we find out that they have furniture payments of $300 per month to a furniture rental store. Again, when asked, they said they could not afford to save up to purchase furniture, another poor choice because simply saving that amount for a year would have given them $3600 to buy furniture. They were down to $1700 left over before living expenses. So we asked how much they spend on groceries and to our surprise, their response was 'very little', because they go out to eat every day. Obviously, another bad decision."

"Oh my!" Sara responded. "That is amazing. They made one bad decision after another which just seemed to compound, they were sort of in a downward spiral."

"That's right." Miss Chris agreed. "Their perspective that they would not have money at the end of the month, became their reality."

"How are they doing now?" Larry asked.

"After working with us, they realized were they could make some different choices and take action including changing some of their beliefs. They put some practices in place and they started to have money left over each month which they could then invest and save. They are actually doing quite well now." Miss Chris assured them.

Coach added, "Changing perspective is the beginning, but you also must put in place some different practices. That is actually our next financial pillar, **Practice**. We should wrap up for the evening and talk about the remaining 2 Pillars the next time we meet. We hope these thoughts about perspectives help you to get going and keep your mind tuned into success. Put them into practice and soon you'll be dialed into success and abundance. Would you like to get together next week?"

"Would we ever, just name the time and place and we will be there!" Larry responded.

QUESTIONS TO PONDER AND ACTIONS TO TAKE

How do perceive yourself?

How do you perceive money?

How do perceive yourself in reference to money?

If you are working to make a living, what do you do, if anything, to maximize that living?

What do expect to have left over at the end of the month?

Are there opportunities for you to reduce your monthly expenses?

Are there opportunities for you to add additional income to your family budget?

Discuss with your spouse the definition of *a lot* of money, including different contexts.

As you talk to people, listen for clues as to what their perspective is about money.

Look at your own life, where do you live today in the CS Triangle? Where would you like to live? What steps can you take to move there?

CHAPTER 6
PRACTICES

We are what we repeatedly do. Excellence, therefore, is not an act but a habit. – Aristotle

"Welcome back!" Miss Chris smiled and said as she opened the front door.

Once again she led them to the back porch and they were seated at the table for dinner. And once again, Coach jumped right into the lesson for the evening. "I want to start tonight by going back to a comment you made at our last get together. I asked if you knew how to get rich and you said yes, by making more money," said Coach.

"Sure I remember," said Larry.

"Let me share this with you. I've made a copy for your folder." Coach handed them a copy or an article. "It is an article I recently read in *Fortune* Magazine entitled 'Why the rich aren't feeling so rich.[8] The article highlights how many are trying so hard but still falling short. The article's author, Shawn Tully, invented a term that is catching on, HENRY. It's an acronym for High Earners, Not Rich Yet. Mr. Tully explains that those we would consider rich, because they make a lot of money, such as doctors and lawyers making $250,000 to $500,000 a year, are not really rich at all. Why? Because Mr. Tully points out, they lose so much money to taxes. Their income is based on the services they provide, rather than passive income from investments. They spend their money on liabilities like homes, instead of on assets that produce cash flow.

"I thought the article was a great lead into what we are going to be discussing tonight. The third pillar of success, our third "P", is **Practice**. Webster defines practice 'to do repeatedly in order to learn or become proficient; make a habit or custom'. In other words, we will cover what the rich *do* that most people do not."

Invest in yourself, only perfect practice makes perfect

Miss Chris chimed in."We purposely made Practice the third pillar and not one of the first two pillars. We have found that most 'financial experts' and 'coaches' like to start with what to do and they do not bother to explain the how and why you should. Without the foundations and understanding of principles and perspectives, the temptation would be for us to just try to tell you what to do. That is much more complicated than it sounds. There are way too many people that believe just do *something* is the answer, even if the something you do is wrong. People also believe that practice makes perfect. Neither cliché is true about money.

"One of my favorite authors is John Wooden. He has a wonderful quote that clarifies our first point about practice. Wooden suggests that we 'don't get activity confused with accomplishment'. Coach chuckled and continued, "There are a lot of people that believe if they just do *something*, everything will work out. We believe that is not only simplistic, it is dangerous and can lead to many stupid financial decisions. We see lots of people that have convinced themselves that they are moving in the right direction because they are doing something. Well, what if you are doing the exact wrong thing, will that make it right? Will it get you closer to your goal? Another Wooden quote is 'only perfect practices makes perfect'. If you did the wrong thing over and over and became good at it, would that make what you were doing right?"

"No, I guess it would make me good at doing the wrong thing, wouldn't it?" Larry suggested.

"You are right. If you got really good at playing the fiddle wrong, it would make you a really bad fiddle player!" Coach exclaimed.

"One of the first things you and Sara need to do is recognize the best investment you can ever make is in yourself. We hope you picked that up from our previous meetings." Miss Chris added.

"We did. It was one of the first Principle you discussed with us, to become lifelong learners and observers." Larry agreed.

"Are we going to learn tonight *how* we invest in ourselves?" Sara asked.

"Yes, we are going to concentrate tonight on the *how* for most of the principles mentioned. So let's start with the first few principles we covered and the practices associated with those principles.

Principle:

- **There are rules and you need to learn them**
- **Become a lifelong learner and observer**
- **Creating wealth starts between your ears; certainty of purpose makes all things possible.**

Practice:
Invest in yourself, only perfect practice makes perfect

"Do you remember the Albert Einstein quote, 'You have to learn the rules of the game. And then you have to play better than anyone else'?" Coach asked.

Larry and Sara nodded. Sara added, "You taught us that many of us are playing the game of life as hard as we can and not getting where we want to. It must mean that either we don't know the rules or we aren't very good at the game."

"That's right." Coach affirmed. "It is our experience that people are trying very hard, so it must the fact that they don't know the rules. There are many ways that you can invest in yourself and learn the *rules*. You may have noticed that Chris and I read a lot, financial materials and all different kinds of books. This is one of the ways you can invest in yourself, reading. You can also go to seminars, listen to talk radio, meet new people, observe successful people, all of these activities are investments in oneself."

Practice: You are what you eat

"The Pillars of Success often overlap. As we learned last time we met, the principles about creating wealth begins between the ears and our personal perspectives about wealth are both related to results. Practices also determine results. As I mentioned before, no one can overestimate the power of the mind and its role in our success. It is imperative to keep our minds right and on the right track if we are to achieve balanced success in our career, finances, health, emotions, relationships and spiritual practices. Remember our analogy of a radio station? We should continually tune into the *Success* station. The only way to hear a radio station is to be tuned into it. Like most radio stations, they play 24 hours a day, 7 days a week. However, if you are even a little off, you cannot get the full effect; instead you get static and distortion. The same is true with our mind and success. If our minds and our thoughts get static or distorted, our success will get sidetracked. As our minds stay tuned to successes, our bodies will then carry out this success and we will begin to experience abundance! We have told our kids since they were born that there are only two things in life that you can control: your attitude and your actions/effort. We break down the practices of tuning into success into the following actions:

Eat right and exercise.

"That's right. I know we are talking about financial success, but the way we eat and the amount of exercise we get goes a long way toward our mind's ability to tune into success. I know,that when I personally go more than a day or so without working out, I get cranky. I wonder if that is why some people are constantly cranky because they have gone weeks or months without working out. Put the right foods into your body and the brain responds. Exercise on a regular basis and the body releases chemicals that literally ignite your brain for success!"

Use your innate ability to decide and choose.

"Success starts with a decision, and so does failure. One of the things that separate us from the animals is that we live by choice, not instinct. Constantly flexing that muscle of choice builds it up and keeps us on track for success. It is like working out. The more we do it correctly, the stronger we get. Remember the quote by Wooden, 'only perfect practice makes perfect'. We need to make sure that we are working out correctly. If you want to keep your mind tuned for success, keep it healthy by making good choices and decisions on a regular basis. For example, do you have a bad habit? Then flex your mind muscle and choose to change, today. If you choose to stay the same way, and those are the only two alternatives, you will have just chosen to tune your mind to a different station than *success.*"

Put good stuff into your brain/ Keep the junk out.

"There are lots of things that want to work their way into our minds, and eventually work themselves out again in our actions. There will be lots that we just get from walking around all day. But what about what we put in on purpose? We can choose to put good stuff in on a regular basis. Do you take time each day to put good things into your mind, to tune into success? Here are two things to consider when you are choosing what to put into your mind. First, ask yourselves these questions. Is it positive? Will it build you up or tear you down? Will it make you a better person? Will you grow from it? Will it tune you into success? Secondly, will it move you toward your goals in the areas of your life that you want to see success and abundance? There will always be junk floating around, like a fellow employee who gripes all the time. But what surprises me is how many people who want success, actually willfully choose to put junk into their minds and then expect to be tuned into success. Evaluate everything that you put into your mind. Evaluate what you read, listen to and watch. We live in a fast-paced world and we have little time. Why then would we spend our precious time putting junk into our minds? Ask yourself, does what you read, listen to and watch move you toward your goals, or away from them? This is the catch. Everyone *wants* success, but not everyone is willing to do what it takes to get it. Are you?"

"Yes we are!" Larry and Sara said in unison.

"We suspected that" Miss Chris smiled. "Otherwise you probably wouldn't have spent your last few Friday nights with us. We are so glad that you have. The next Practice we suggest is that you:

Practice: Know the times

"If you recall when we were talking about Perspective, we quoted Charles Dickens 'It was the best of times it was the worst of times'.

Coach jumped in and finished the quote "'it was the age of wisdom, it was the age of foolishness, it was the epoch of belief, it was the epoch of incredulity, it was the season of Light, it was the season of Darkness, it was the spring of hope, it was the winter of despair, we had everything before us, we had nothing before us, we were all going direct to heaven, we were all doing direct the other way'. Isn't it amazing that something written 150 years ago so accurately describes the current world economy and our own economic situation over the past couple of years? We have certainly seen the worst economic times in our lifetime. On March 9, 2009, the Dow bottomed out at 6,547, less than half its value only a year earlier. Think about it, the entire net worth of American industry shrunk by half in less than 12 months. Yet, since March 9, 2009, we have seen some of the best of times on Wall Street as the Dow rose a meteoric 50% in value in less than 6 months. But most of us live on Main Street, not Wall Street. What does all this mean for us as parents, business people and entrepreneurs?"

Larry and Sara both shrugged. They were enjoying the education.

Coach continued, "I ask these questions because another practice that I like to include under investing in yourself, is the practice of *knowing the times*, staying current on what is happening in the world today.

"In one of the best books I've read recently, 'Increase Your Financial IQ' by Robert Kiyosaki, the author gives a brief human history and then concludes with differentiating information and knowledge. Let me share a couple of his points, he wrote about the four economic ages of humanity. They are:

The Hunter-Gatherer Age: In the Hunter-Gatherer Age, humans relied on nature to provide wealth. They were nomadic and went where the hunting was good and the vegetation plentiful. You had to know how to hunt and to gather, or you died. For the hunter-gatherer, the tribe was social security. Socioeconomically, everyone was even. They were all poor.

The Agrarian Age: The Agrarian Age saw the rise of classes between people. Due to the development of technology to plant and cultivate the land, those who owned the land became royalty, and those who worked it became peasants. The royals rode horses, while the peasants walked.

Socioeconomically there were two groups, the rich and the poor.

The Industrial Age: While many people would place the beginning of the Industrial Age in the 1800s with the rise of factories, I actually think of it as beginning in 1492 with Columbus. When Columbus struck out to find the New World, it was to find new sources of valuable resources such as oil, copper, tin and rubber. During this time the value of real estate shifted from growing crops to providing resources. This led to the land becoming even more valuable. And three classes emerged: the rich, the middle-class, and the poor. The rich figured out ways to leverage resources, thus, we have Rockefeller and oil, and Carnegie and steel.

The Information Age: Today, we are in the Information Age, where information leveraged by technology and inexpensive resources like silicon, produce wealth. This means that the price of getting wealthy has gone down. For the first time in history, wealth is available to just about everyone. There are now four groups of people: the poor, the middle-class, the rich, and the super rich."

Opportunities exist

"If you make it a practice to be aware of current events and the times we live in, you will be more likely to see opportunities that exist to make money. Let me give you an example, have you seen the movie about the founder of Facebook, Mark Zuckerberg called *The Social Network*?"

Sara indicated that they had not.

"The movie highlights one of major successes of the Information Age. It was reported recently in the *New York Times* that Facebook has struck a deal with Goldman Sachs and others to raise $500 million dollars in additional funding. A number of Goldman clients received an email from their Goldman broker, offering them the opportunity to invest in an unnamed private company that is considering a transaction to raise additional capital. Another person briefed on the deal said that Goldman clients would have to pony up a minimum of $2 million to invest and would be prohibited from selling their shares until 2013. But the Goldman spokesman declined to comment.

"Facebook has raised $500 million from Goldman Sachs and a Russian investor in a transaction that values the company at $50 billion, according to people involved in the transaction. As part of its deal with Facebook, Goldman is expected to raise as much as $1.5 billion from investors for Facebook. With a website valued at $50 billion. And an estimated net worth of $13.5 billion. CEO, Mark Zuckerberg is now part of the super rich. Not bad for a 26-year old college dropout.

"In my travels, I've literally seen local people texting on their cell phones while riding on the back of a donkey cart. In classrooms all across the world the Internet is readily available and technology is second nature to most kids. Regardless of socioeconomic class, information is largely free and abundant. For the first time in history, people can access information and learn about anything no matter whether they are rich or poor."

Knowledge is Key

"While information is valuable, it's not as valuable as knowledge. Knowledge gives you the ability to filter out unimportant information to find the important information. Knowledge gives you the power to act on information. Knowledge is what makes you rich, not information. You could have all the information in the world, but without knowledge, you would still be poor. There are a lot of smart, poor people. The reason Mark Zuckerberg is such a success is because he has knowledge of what to do with information and knowledge of how to build technologies to leverage information.

"As I view it, Mark Zuckerberg has knowledge of Internet technology and computer programming that enabled him to build Facebook. He also knows how to build a team and find people smarter than him to make Facebook bigger and better. Finally, he has knowledge that information is valuable for selling. Facebook excels at collecting your information, processing it, and selling it to advertisers who target their ads to make money off of you.

"It is not the information that makes Mark Zuckerberg rich, it's his ability to process and leverage it. That takes knowledge. And knowledge comes from education."

Larry responded, "Amidst the gloomy economic news that gives me hope. We live in an age where wealth is abundant and accessible by everyone, including Sara and I. But we have to be educated to be able to process and leverage it. We appreciate you taking the time to start that education!"

"You are very welcome. It is also good for Chris and I to continue to educate people, because it helps us stay up with the times as well. As long as we are talking about the practice of *knowing the times* which helps us see opportunities, let me ask you a question. What do think caused the Recession of 2008?" Coach asked.

"I know that Lehman Brothers' collapse is listed as the origin, but I guess I don't know what caused that. I remember reading about greed on Wall Street and how congress worked back room deals with Freddie Mac and Fannie Mae, approving transactions that were not financially responsible," Larry responded.

Innovation Stagnation

"Let me give you a brief history lesson on our economy. Many people blame today's financial crisis on Wall Street. However, once the crisis had begun, the crash on Main Street was caused by consumers realizing that many of the products and services they were buying were simply not worth their cost. The same house that sold for $250,000 in 1999, was nine years older in 2008, and not worth $450,000, although that was what it was on the market for. Yet many home-buyers were willing to pay that much for it, due to easy credit and a fear that prices would keep rising.

"A new car with the same features as last year's model did not justify an annual price increase, especially in the summer of 2008, when gasoline reached $5 per gallon and consumers wanted more fuel-efficient vehicles. And no mass-produced handbag was really worth $10,000 or more. When consumers rebelled in 2008 against paying more for the same or less, businesses were forced to cut their costs. Employers worldwide laid-off millions of employees and blamed it on the recession.

"In the 20th century, America grew to become the world's greatest economy because of entrepreneurial innovations. Examples include Henry Ford (cars), Abraham Levitt (homes) and Steve Jobs (iPods, iPhones); all great 20th century innovators. Entrepreneurs created new products and services and ultimately created entire industries so compelling that consumers *had* to have them. Each of these new products and services created entire industries of support products, such as gas stations, restaurants, furnishings, cell phones, iTunes, the App Store and the list goes on. There is an old circular question that asks 'is need the mother of invention or is it that invention is the mother of need'? Regardless, Americans wanted to work harder than ever to purchase items that had not even existed when they were born. The other day I asked my 19 year old grandson if he had ever used a payphone or a phone book to look up a number. He asked me why anyone would use a payphone since everyone had a cell phone and why use a phone book since they could look up any number as well as directions online.

"Let's take a look at two of the fundamentals of the US economy: house and cars. The average and median price of a single-family home rose from $180,000 in 1999 to $300,000 in 2008. It was essentially the same house, except it was nine years older and had an outdated kitchen. The average home size increased steadily from 1,200 square feet in 1960 to 2,300 square feet in 2001. Each year, houses included more useful features, such as built-in air conditioning or better insulation, but size and quality stagnated from 2001 to 2008, only the price increased.

"The average price of a new automobile in the United States rose 40 percent, from about $20,000 in 1999 to $28,000 in 2008, without any significant increase in quality, performance or features. In the all-important area of fuel efficiency, performance actually declined from 17 to 16 miles per gallon in these years, after having increased consistently every year before 1998 from 12 mpg in 1975 to 17 mpg in 1997.

"I vividly remember each new automobile my father bought in the 1960s and why it was superior to the car it replaced. Air conditioning, automatic transmission, power windows, seat belts, the list goes on and on for the compelling new features that came out with each model year. If you didn't purchase a new car for a new feature, you purchased a new car because it cost less. You could actually save money over the cost of maintaining your existing vehicle.

"For entrepreneurs today, the last decade of innovation stagnation has created the greatest economic opportunity in history because there are so many ready-to-be-implemented advances in virtually every sector of our economy. The greatest personal fortunes of 2020 are about to be created by entrepreneurs who either lower the price of existing products or introduce new products and services to our economy."

"Amazing," Sara said as she finished jotting down the notes from all the information they were covering. "I remember *innovation* and *risk taking* are both the characteristics of the wealthy mindset, we will definitely start educating ourselves about the current market and times so we can be prepared to recognize opportunities. What other facts about the current times can we learn tonight?"

Saving Money – Saving vs. Investing

"I'm glad you brought up the characteristics of wealthy mindsets we covered. Do you remember that another one of the characteristics of the working mindset was savers? Savers systematically follow behaviors of the majority and may not even realize that their behavior is based on emotion rather than a conscious decision. The Wealthy Mindset, on the other hand, is characterized by investing. We will talk about investments in a few minutes. Beforehand, let me continue with a little more of a history lesson as it relates to saving.

"When I was a young man about your age there was a premium placed upon saving our money. Of course times and economics were different. Personal credit cards did not exist as they do today. We had just survived WWII and the Great Depression. People saved. Today, well let's take a look at some of the numbers."

Coach handed them another article. "Before we get into this article, let's define a few terms:

Disposable Income: Personal Income less Personal Current Taxes

Personal Saving: Disposable Personal Income less Personal Outlays

Personal Saving Rate: (Personal Saving / Disposable Personal Income) * 100

Note: Personal outlays will include such things as food, housing and transportation in addition to interest payments on non-mortgage debt and transfer payments to government or social services.

"The US Department of Commerce: Bureau of Economic Analysis (BEA) has data on the personal savings rate of the average American dating from January 1st, 1959 until present day. Now let's look at the historical trend of personal savings rates in the United States.

"In the first month that the BEA provided the data, January 1959, the personal savings rate in the United States was 8.3%. This means that, on average, Americans were able to save 8.3% of their disposable incomes.

"For the next decade or so, the personal savings rate remained more or less the same, in the range of 7.5% - 8.5%. Before inundating you with numbers, let's think about what they mean. If the personal savings rate was about 8% that means that on the average people were saving and not spending $8 of every $100 they made. If you compare that today which is very close to $0, and in some cases below $0, I think you can begin to see the problem and understand that the issues that you are facing are not unique - you are not alone.

"In the early 70s, the average savings rate started to spike, hitting a peak of 14.6% in May of 1975. The spike in personal savings rates from 1973 to 1975 coincided with the deep recession that was ravaging the country over the same period of time. You may remember gas lines, and people paying double digit interest rates for their home mortgages. As you can see, recessions usually result in increased personal savings rates as people tend to dramatically scale back on their purchases in times of economic distress.

"After spiking in the mid 70's, the savings rate started to fall once the country pushed through the recession. By the late 70s, the rate had fallen to almost half of what is was just

94

5 years before to 7.9%, before starting to trend higher once again. Why? You guessed it, another recession.

"The recession of the early 80s was a particularly nasty mix of high inflation and weak economic activity, the media even coined a new term: *stagflation*. The average savings rate spiked to 12.2% in November of 1981, which was right when the national unemployment rate in the country really started to trend higher. The average savings rate pulled back when the economy started to recover, spiked over 10% once again in 1984, and then really started to noticeably pull back in the mid 80s. Consumer confidence was rapidly improving in the country, Ronald Reagan swept to victory on the back of a strengthening economy, and people were starting to spend their money once again. It was *morning* in America.

"There was another recession in the early 90s, but no noticeable increase in the average savings rate. As a matter of fact, the savings rate of the average American held steady during the recession of the early 90s, and then proceeded to fall like a stone throughout the rest of the decade.

"By January 2000, the average savings rate was 3.5% - it would end up falling below 1.0% multiple times between 2000 and 2010. When the economy nearly collapsed in 2008, the savings rate started to trend higher, moving from 1.3% in January of 2008 to 4.2% in December of 2009. Why the dramatic drop in the average rate of savings between 1990 and 2008?"

Larry and Sara realized it was rhetorical question, they nodded as Coach continued.

"The mindset of the average US consumer changed. There was greater access to credit and increasingly sophisticated marketing campaigns that had people cracking open their wallets or purses in droves. Due to the surge of available credit, many people actually maintained negative savings rates. I'm sure that we all have known somebody who has spent more than what they made, this was all made possible through the explosion of available credit.

"This access to credit made people want to spend, and marketers exploited this to the nth degree. People were flush with cash (and credit) in the post 9-11 economy. Interest rates were low, the real estate market was strong and many people were in a mood to spend. And spend they did.

"TV shows and commercials and Internet advertising campaigns were bombarding us 24/7 with images that appealed to our materialism. We took the bait and spent money like we had never spent it before, completely abandoning the thrifty mindset of the prior generation. People ended up overextended due to way too much easy credit being dished out, and the economy fell flat on its face in 2008.

"The average savings rate, which had plummeted to basically zero, now started to rebound as people stressed about their financial futures. It's pretty simple, when people are feeling good about their circumstances, they spend more.

When people are worried about their futures, they save more.

"Access to credit has been significantly pared back in the United States since the beginning of the recession in December of 2007. If the national unemployment numbers continue to stay high over the next year or two, and there is no reason to think that they won't, then it will be interesting to see how the average personal savings rate will respond.

"However, I mentioned that these numbers represent the majority. The wealthy mindset following the principles we have outlined and they behave differently. Let's switch gears and talk about another couple of principle we discussed on our first night:

Principle:

- **Employment has changed; create other means of revenue Focus on assets/own a business**

- **You must accumulate assets and assets are not necessarily what you think**

"Whether you are rich now, on your way to being rich, or just thinking about it, most of us have fantasized about what it would be like for money, or rather lack of it, not to be a problem. Most people stay in the realm of fantasy, maybe dipping out occasionally to buy a lottery ticket. Another group, not satisfied with the 9 to 5 grind, take a few more risks and they pour their energy into business ideas, opportunities and beginning companies. Most will fail within three to five years. There are a lot of obstacles along the way. The system is designed to be tough. Is it easy to lose weight? Is it easy to quit smoking? As we have discussed, most accomplishments are an uphill climb. But if you learn to invest in yourself, which by the way is a life-long endeavor, the next practice we suggest is that you work toward owning some sort of business or money generating asset."

"But you just said that most will fail," Larry interjected.

"Yes, but one of the big differences, as you and Sara have learned working with us, is your focus and intention."

Focus Intention – Making Money

"Most of your friends have the focus or intention of making a living, or if they are more ambitious, perhaps a good living. But if you look at results, how many rich people are employees? How many wealthy people, those in the Forbes 400 list, have jobs or even good jobs?

"The Principles, Perspective and Practices that we outline helps focus your intention so we can talk about millionaire success strategies. The basics help, but the intention has to come from the simplest truth. When going into business, do not go halfway. You could, but would that be much better than working a typical job? When we are talking about our wealth creation blueprints, the reason why we go into business and the reason we buy assets have to be drawn into the foundation. It is so simple and powerful, yet not very well understood. With an understanding that you are in business to make money will help you keep your focus when the inevitable challenges, disappointments and setbacks arise. Let's remember you are doing this because you are going to be rich! Whatever other intentions you have, whether you want to provide for your family, want the ability to buy nice things, desire to travel, to be an artist or to help the poor. Whatever other intentions you have, they do not have to conflict with the simple truth that you are in business to make money.

"Let's do a quick comparison. Suppose you and your friends from work get together, what do you talk about?"

"We would probably talk about how we could get a raise, how we could improve the conditions at our company, how we could get some more hours, things like that." replied Larry.

"I would suggest that there would also be a little animosity," volunteered Sara. "Some of your coworkers are bitter about your boss and the ownership. They believe they are entitled to more, and that it is not fair that the owners are making more money than they do."

"Okay, good. Now, what do you think a group of my associates would discuss?" asked Coach.

"Well, uh, uh, I guess I don't know," stuttered Larry. He had not even considered the fact that Coach and his associates would brainstorm business ideas.

"Most people say their financial goal is to make money. That is a good goal, but it is not specific enough. If you have wishy-washy intentions, you are going to get wishy-washy results. If you were to drop in on one of my meetings, we would probably be focused on one of three intentions. These are what we call the practices of the rich."

Practice: Income Strategies

"My associates share strategies about making income, just like you and your friends, however we will take it two steps further and discuss the passive income component and economic value. The practices we focus on are:

1) Creating a high working income
2) Creating a passive, residual income
3) Enhancing the economic value of our company

"Remember, a business is not a job. A business is too much work with too many challenges to be defined as simply a vehicle to earn a decent living," explained Coach. "Owning a business and owning assets should be designed to be a vehicle to set you free and create nothing short of wealth. Most broke people have struggles, because they put most of their energy and attention into *job security*, which is one of the biggest oxymoron that exists. Instead they should be focusing and putting their energy into buying, creating, and selling assets."

Practice:

You must accumulate assets
and assets are not necessarily what you think...

"The statistics are staggering about those that work their entire lives and then have to keep working because the *assets* they have accumulated aren't really *assets*. Let me share this:"

Your house is NOT your biggest Asset

"Recently, I read a great article by Barbara Kiviat entitled *The Case against Home Ownership* published in *TIME* magazine.[7] In my opinion Ms. Kiviat rightly identifies that the myth of your house being an asset has contributed greatly to our current financial crisis. She quotes:

> *But the dark side of home ownership is now all too apparent: foreclosures and walkaways, neighborhoods plagued by abandoned properties and plummeting home values, a nation in which families have $6 trillion less in housing wealth than they did just three years ago. Indeed, easy lending stimulated by the cult of home ownership may have triggered the financial crisis and led directly to its biggest bailout, that of Fannie Mae and Freddie Mac [...] for the better part of a century, politics, industry and culture aligned to create a fetish of the idea of buying a house.*

"The article went on to quote some numbers:

- Almost $6 trillion in housing wealth has been lost since 2005

- Home values have dropped 30 percent

- Existing home sales dropped 27 percent over the previous month

- Housing inventories stand at 12.5 months, over twice what's considered healthy

"With numbers like these, I can see why people such as Ms. Kiviat are realizing that the American dream of becoming wealthy through home ownership is one of the biggest lies ever perpetrated on the US public. Unfortunately for many, hindsight is 20/20. That is why it is imperative to know what an asset really is and not just believe what *they* say it is.

"But that was what I was always taught! Isn't that the American dream? What are we supposed to do?" Larry said, exasperated.

"The path to wealth is one of constant learning and toil. Though I've often been accused of *get rich quick* schemes, the real message is one of continual financial education and of acquiring cash flowing assets over the course of your entire life. Security does not come from hoping prices go up, but from being financially intelligent enough to search for, find, and acquire solid assets that provide income every month for a lifetime. That is not easy. It is not quick. And it is not something the ordinary person can do if they rely on the education they received in school. As long as we are talking about real assets; what do you believe is your biggest asset?" Coach asked.

"I know it is not my checkbook or stock account," Larry replied.

"Based on what I am hearing from you and Miss Chris, perhaps it is our willingness to learn and grow," Sara added.

"You are close Sara. In our opinion your biggest asset is *time* and more importantly how you use your time." said Coach.

Your biggest asset is Time

"Here are a couple of things that we have learned about time. All of us have the same amount of time per day. None of us know how many of those days we are given. What matters is how we use each day that we are given. Have you ever noticed that people answer the question 'how are you doing' with the word *busy*."

"Sure, that is because everyone is, right Coach?" replied Larry

"I don't think so," responded Coach. "How do you think Bill Gates or Warren Buffet would respond to that question? Do you think they would respond that they are *busy*? No, I don't think that they would. I think there are two main reasons that most people respond this way. The first is that it is socially acceptable to be busy today and there is an emotional acceptance to being busy. The second is that most people don't control their own time and their own lives. It is interesting to me that the janitor in Warren Buffet's plant is busier in his mind than Warren Buffet

103

actually is. Warren Buffet feels that he controls a little more of his life than the janitor, therefore he would probably not answer that question the same way. Wasting this most valuable asset will result in a lifetime of regrets; if you use it well you will experience life to its fullest."

Larry and Sara nodded as they continued to take notes.

"As we mentioned before, it is highly unusual for someone to work for one employer their entire life. We actually know lots of people that believe you should have multiple things going on at the same time."

"That's right, Miss Chris. We also believe in the practice that we must:

Practice: Pay yourself First

"When you get paid, put something aside for yourself before you pay your obligations. That is a mistake that most people make. What do you guys think about *that* practice?"

"We have tried to do that, but we always seem to need the money we save and we never seem to be able to get ahead," replied Sara.

"I think that it is easy for the two of you to do that because you are rich and it does not take everything you make just to live," Larry added.

Coach sat back and listened carefully and responded, "I hear what you are saying, but ask yourself a question, what comes first the habits or the results? Do you think we are wealthy because we pay ourselves first or do you think we learned how to pay ourselves first and now we are wealthy? As we stated before, one of the key financial principles is that financial skills should be an inherent part of our human experience. From birth until death, we face needs and challenges we must meet and overcome. Our confidence, self-esteem and the ability to contribute are dependent upon our willingness to improve ourselves in general and our financial skills in particular.

"I know it can be frustrating to learn and start applying these principles, perspectives and practices. We believe that deciding what you want and then getting started in this is one of the most powerful lessons in life. You two have obviously reached a point where you have not been getting what you want and frustration has started to form. That's good! I guess there is another practice you can write down."

Practice: Frustration is a positive, not a negative

"Frustration is positive because it is what will drive you to the next level."

"Frustration is good?" Larry questioned with a tinge of skepticism.

"Oh yes," replied Coach. "Let's take a look at some of your associates from work. Are they so frustrated with their lives that they are doing something about it?"

"Well, no, no one is as frustrated as Sara and I," Larry agreed.

"Exactly. Are any of your friends here on Friday night with their notebooks? Are any of them reading books or going to seminars to improve their situations? Are any of your friends asking the questions that you are asking? Obviously, the answer is no. I believe that it is your level of frustration that is driving you to do something. That is why I said frustration is good. Most of your friends and unfortunately most people today may be frustrated, but they don't choose to take action. But you have decided to take action."

"I have a question. How do we manage our time and lives opposed to letting it manage us?" asked Sara.

"Great question, once again Sara. To make the best use of time at work, just as in our lives, we must first identify our goals and prioritize our tasks according to their importance and from there, establish time-lines. When given the option to establish time-lines, we should carefully consider the full scope of the project or task in light of our other obligations before committing to a deadline. We must then establish a working balance between the tasks and the resources as well as our ability to perform those tasks with excellence. Notice I said with *excellence* not perfection. Life is about doing things with excellence, not perfection. This is a perfect lead-in to our next practice that is related to some principles we outlined:

Principle:
There is a price to pay for Financial Success,
the price of regret or discipline.

Practice: You need a plan; Set Goals

"Some projects are relatively simple and require minimal planning but others like your financial future are more complex and require significant planning. Planning your financial future means identifying and prioritizing goals in the form of tasks that will help achieve your goals. All of us have resources to draw from in achieving our goals, and we must have ways to periodically measure how far we have come in achieving those plans.

"There is a saying 'if you don't have goals, you always hit the target.' Goal setting is just a variation on project planning. In each case, we must:

- Identify your goals and desired results
- Identify time needed to accomplish the goal
- Identify and organize the resources available
- Identify and complete tasks in order to meet the goals and desired results

"Keep in mind that you will probably miss your goals on numerous occasions. That is okay, it is part of the growth process. I remember as a young man, I was always setting my goals in such a way that I could easily hit them because I was so afraid of failing. Now I recognize that failing in your attempt is not failure. The only real failure is not getting back up. Two of my favorite quotes from people I consider very successful are: Henry Ford who said 'Failure is simply the opportunity to begin again, this time more intelligently'. Winston Churchill said 'Success is not final, failure is not fatal: it is the courage to continue that counts'. We have covered the importance of courage and breaking out of fear as one of the Financial Success Principles. Now let's go through some more practices that we have learned over the years:

Practice: Retirement planning

"Recently, February 19 of this year, *The Wall Street Journal* featured an article entitled *Boomers Find 401(k) Plans Come Up Short*. Here was the second line in the article: 'The 401(k) generation is beginning to retire, and it isn't a pretty sight.'

"Here are some other interesting quotes from the article that explain why retirement for the boomers is so ugly.

> *"The median household headed by a person aged 60 to 62 with a 401(k) account has less than one-quarter of what is needed in that account to maintain its standard of living in retirement."*

"The government changed the rules of retirement in 1974 with the passage of the Employee Retirement Income Security Act (ERISA) of 1974. This eventually became referred to as the 401(k) act, because it paved the way for that retirement investment vehicle.

"One of the biggest problems with the 401(k) is that it requires people with no financial education to be in charge of their retirement investing. Because people had no financial education, a whole new industry was created, financial planning. The problem with financial planners is that they're sales people, not investors. They push the products of their employers, usually paper assets."

"That is so true!" exclaimed Larry. "My financial planner is no better off than I am; he is just always trying to sign me up for this or that. And at my workplace they have education meetings to try to teach us what to with this plan they give us, but most of the time it feels like they are talking over our heads but no one ever asks any questions because most of us don't know what to ask. I hear terms I don't understand like blue chip stocks, dividend reinvestment, 12B-1 fees and stuff like that. What they need is a 401(k) for dummies book."

"You make a couple of great points about the investment world and the average working person. But I have to disagree with one point, I don't think we need the dummies book because I don't think most Americans are dummies. I think that they are undereducated financially and some of that is on purpose.

"The 401(k) is a defined contribution (DC) plan, meaning that you put money into it for your retirement. Prior to that, most people had defined benefit (DB) plans, meaning your employer paid for your retirement and your healthcare for the rest of your life.

"While the rules of retirement changed in 1974, most people's mindset didn't. They still played by the old rules of money. Remember what Einstein said about learning the rules of the game and then learning to play better than anyone else? Most Americans that choose to save money for retirement think that putting a little aside in a 401(k) would be enough. Unfortunately, they do not understand the powers of inflation, taxes, and debt; and how the market works. Many people have lost a lot of money in their 401(k) plans because they had no control over their money, giving it to financial planners, former teachers, plumbers, waiters, etc., who became sales people for the financial industry. Today, as the *Wall Street Journal* article points out, the result of this is a devastating realization that retirement is not an option, at least not at the standard of living many expect.

"Here's another quote from the same article: '*Even counting Social Security and any pensions or other savings, most 401(k) participants appear to have insufficient savings. Facing shortfalls, many people are postponing retirement, moving to cheaper housing, buying less-expensive food, cutting back on travel, taking bigger risks with their investments and making sacrifices they never imagined.*' "

"That feels like us," Sara said. "We feel that we have a very real retirement crisis happening right now. We don't have enough savings to retire even with a 401(k), Social Security, a pension, and savings. We also feel we are financially ignorant which is obviously why we are here."

"You are not alone," Coach agreed. "In a new poll taken of people ages 44 to 75, more than three in five (61 percent) said they fear depleting their assets more than they fear dying.

"Katie Libbe, Vice President of consumer marketing for Allianz Life Insurance Company of North America, the company that conducted the poll of 3,257 people quoted; 'One of the things in the study that was surprising to us was the level of fear among respondents'. [10]

"With people living longer, we're challenged to extend retirements that could last 20 to 30 years or more. There was a time that the average retired person lived a couple of years after he retired. Over the last generation, the number of private sector workers with traditional pensions has declined significantly. Health care and other costs in retirement keep rising.

"Add it up, and it means people today shoulder more personal responsibility to finance longer and more expensive retirements. This calls for a fundamental shift in the way we plan for retirement, from just accumulating savings to planning for lifetime income.

"As I have spoken around the country, I have observed that there is a general feeling of fear when it comes to finances. The fear seems to get worse when I question people about what they are going to do about it. So we need to ask NOW WHAT? What are you doing that is working and you need to do more of? What are you doing that you need to quit doing and do something else? It is one thing to 'know', it is another thing entirely to do.

"The real problem is that people train themselves to live paycheck to paycheck, buying more liabilities as their earned income goes up. Though they know the old advice of live below their means, most people do not follow it. Instead, they have so many liabilities that they cannot retire, and are forced to live below their means, making cuts they never hoped to make and selling properties they thought were assets but found out the hard way were liabilities," explained Coach.

"Chris and I have learned another way. We don't believe in living below our means. We think that crushes our spirit. Instead, we buy assets that pay for our liabilities. The difference between Chris and I, and the people struggling at retirement is that those people play by the old rules of money, relying on savings and the 401(k) for retirement. The problem is that people are living longer, healthcare is more expensive, and those savings are not enough. Yet, they have no other way to have money come in besides going back to work and making cuts in expenses. Further, they have passed up opportunities earlier in their life because they didn't see them or did not want to see them and now they believe it is too late."

Investing

"But isn't that the ultimate Catch-22?" asked Larry. "I mean how can we invest in businesses or opportunities, if we don't have any extra cash because we are living paycheck to paycheck? What kind of opportunities can I even afford? I can't buy real estate or oil wells. I can't think of any opportunities that we have even seen; can you Sara?"

"I am not sure I would even know how to recognize an opportunity if it was presented to me," Sara agreed.

"What a great point you guys have just made. If you think that an opportunity is going to come knocking and present itself in a nice package with neon lights and glitter, I think you have a misperception of opportunity.

"Chris and I, on the other hand, invest in opportunities which we call assets that generate cash flow like real estate, oil wells, businesses, and more. Each month, cash comes into our accounts from these investments, covering our expenses. We never say, 'We can't afford that'. We always ask, 'How can we afford that?' We then find an investment that will pay for our standard of living. The difference is our money works for us, not the other way around. Listen to this quote:

"In the stock-market collapses of 2000-2002 and 2007-2009, most people were over-invested in stocks. Some bailed out after the market collapse, suffering on the way down and then missing the rebound."

"This is a tragedy. I mentioned earlier, ERISA forced people who had no financial education to become investors. One of the major problems is that when the markets started down, which they will do, a lot of people panicked and starting selling their holdings and causing the market to fall further, encouraging more fear. This left people financially and emotionally vulnerable. New products were introduced to 'solve' peoples' needs. Products such as: no money down mortgages and home equity loans. Add to this the con-men and crooks that swooped in, taking the form of trusted financial advisers, and sold people on these and other products. The problem is that these financial advisers and planners are not investors either; they are employees of the financial industry. They push their company's products. During the booms, many planners pushed people into the stock market, collecting fees and commissions. People poured their money into the market at the peak, turning it over to the 'experts'. Then the market crashed. 'Invest for the long term, hold steady', the financial planners said. Finally, in a panic, as the market collapsed, people moved their money into bonds and other 'safe' investments. Have you ever wondered why two 'experts' with theoretically the same information and same access to data can make two entirely different recommendations?"

Larry and Sara realized this was another rhetorical question so they encouraged Coach to continue.

"Leery of the stock market, they watched helplessly as the market climbed back up again and bonds paid some of the lowest returns in history. The problem is that people were investing for capital gains, not cash flow. They were hoping to time the market right and cash in on rising prices. That is not investing. It's trading."

"Now, these people are reaching retirement age. These amateur investors, who invested for capital gains, hope they can time the market with no education. Now they are forced to keep working because they lost all their money. Recently, Vanguard has begun urging people to 'contribute' 12% to

15%, including employer contribution, into their 401(k) because of the stock market's weak returns and uncertainty about the future of Social Security and Medicare. This is financial insanity! Einstein defined insanity as is doing the same thing over and over again and expecting different results. The peak of financial ignorance would be to put more money into your 401(k) just because Vanguard or Fidelity or Chase or Merrill Lynch tells you to, especially since, by their own words, the stock market has weak returns!"

Coach was obviously very passionate about this discussion.

Larry related "I've seen some commercials on TV with one of the insurance companies and baby boomers texting each other about their financial futures. One I remember has one of their friends moving in with their kids, and the question comes back 'that won't be us, will it?' Another commercial discusses being on the right path, just one step at a time. I always wondered 'how many steps and how big they are?' Do you know what I'm talking about and can you provide any guidance here Coach?"

"Oh I know what you are talking about and as I mentioned, they are trying to sell us financial security through their own products. A more financially intelligent move would be to invest in your financial education, take back control of your money instead of giving it over to Vanguard and other mutual fund companies who collect fees whether the fund goes up or down. Then begin investing in assets that produce cash flow.

"Unfortunately, for many people it is too late. They do not have the time to build their ark, and I'm afraid that more and more people from my generation, the boomers, will have to work well into their 70s and 80s, sell their houses and cars, and move in with their kids."

"So, the question today is: Are you ready for retirement? Now is the time to begin building your financial ark to survive the coming retirement storm.

Where is the money

"Let me ask you a question, how many places does your money go on a monthly basis?"

"You mean what we spend our money on?" questioned Sara.

"Yes," replied Coach.

Sara answered, "Well, we pay 1 mortgage payment, 2 car payments, 2 credit card bills, insurance, utilities, and groceries. We live pretty frugally. We watch what we spend our money on. I spend some time looking for coupons and sales. We try to save a little for the next rainy day."

"This is where the 4 Pillars we are teaching are all really connected. You and Larry have shared, with us that is, that strategy is not working for you. Let me have you look at your income and expenses a little differently. For every dollar that comes in to your household there are only three places that money goes. The first is taxes. There are a lot of strategies to legally reduce your taxes and I would suggest that you get some advice on that subject. The second place your dollar goes is to living expenses, the mortgage, cars, etc, that we discussed previously. The third is wealth accumulation. Some portion of your dollar should be going there for retirement and buying income generating assets." explained Coach.

"That is the problem!" Larry exclaimed, "we have nothing left over."

"Is that because you start at the wrong place that you end up in the wrong place?" asked Coach. "Why don't we have this be a little homework for the two of you and we'll meet again to discuss the final Pillar, People, next week."

QUESTIONS TO PONDER AND ACTIONS TO TAKE

Write down your dreams, hopes, and ambitions. Sketch out a time-line for how and when you may achieve some or all of them. Most people don't spend time dreaming while others lack the discipline needed to achieve them. With a little planning and discipline, you may surprise yourself. Don't put this off forever or it will never take shape.

Estimate your annual retirement living expenses. Remember, you will probably spending less than you do now. A general rule of thumb is that most people spend about 70% of what they spend before retirement.

Determine your income streams (rental income, social security, residual income, dividend income, etc.)

Gather your important documents. Those should include: checking, CD's, and saving account information, credit card statements, retirement account statement for 401K, IRA, and company pension information, mortgage statements, brokerage account information, insurance statements. Most people have multiple accounts in multiple places, so take some time to gather, it may be a pleasant surprise. Also remember, most of your accounts are accessible online.

Remember, retirement, or at least aging, will happen with or without your financial planning.

Write down a budget of where your money goes on a monthly basis. Now do your budget again putting in the three areas:

118

1) taxes 2) lifestyle expenses 3) wealth accumulation. What is the % in each? What would you like them to be?

Make a list of thoughts, fears, dreams you have about money. Try to categorize them as empowering or limiting.

Meditate on and discuss with your spouse about how any limiting perspectives can be changed to empower.

Ask yourself better questions, you will get better answers. Instead of asking, why does my life stink, or, how come the Jones have more? Ask what makes you joyful? What are you thankful for? What makes you happy at work and home?

Are there opportunities for you to take advantage of your monthly expenses? List them and maximize them.

Are there opportunities for you to add additional income to your family budget? List them and maximize them.

CHAPTER 7
PEOPLE

My success was due to good luck, hard work, and support and advice from friends and mentors. But most importantly, it depended on me to keep trying after I had failed.
-- Mark Warner

Larry and Sara woke up excited. They were going on a picnic with Coach and Miss Chris and they wanted to do something special for them. But how do you give something nice to someone that has everything? The discussion went back and forth about what to do. Larry and Sara were in agreement that they wanted to do something, but the question came down to what?

They decided on picture of their family framed with a note thanking Coach and Miss Chris for putting them on the right financial road that for the first time in either of their memories, filled them with hope and opportunity.

As Sara and Larry arrived, they were surprised to see a convertible out front with Coach and Miss Chris obviously waiting for them.

"Hop in" said Miss Chris, "We have a surprise for you."

As they drove away, Larry and Sara looked at each other, excited to be surrounded by such great people and the luxury of a first class automobile that that could only dream about. As they drove to the ocean the houses became nicer and nicer, Larry asked Sara is they should pinch each other to see if all this was real. They pulled up to a mini mansion right on the beach. Coach and Miss Chris got out and shouted back, "are you guys coming in?"

Larry and Sara ran to catch up and they all walked in the back door together.

"WOW, we didn't know you had another home," gasped Larry.

"This is our little getaway," said Miss Chris, "But it is also an asset. It is paid for and we rent it out to others during the year for additional income."

They settled themselves on the back porch overlooking the ocean. This was a beautiful spot. As with their other meetings, Coach got right to it. "Do you have any questions from what we have shared so far?"

"As we were reflecting on the information that you have shared with us, we were awestruck by the number of books

122

you have read, you have quoted Einstein, Dickens, Wooden, Kiyosaki among others. You shared the success stories of Zuckerberg. How do know so much?" Sara asked.

"As we have shared with you, the first principles and practice we went over was how THE best investment you can make is in yourself is your own education. Reading is one way that we do that. We also like to read about people, you can learn so much from the experiences of others. In fact, that is the final Pillar or "P" we will discuss today - **PEOPLE**. Coach replied.

"In our view it is all about people. The world is full of them, some good, some not so good. Some kind, others not so kind; some optimistic, others pessimistic. There is no denying that developing skills to deal with all kinds of people is imperative in your growth." Coach continued.

"We like to break the discussion we have around this "P", People, into lessons that we have learned over the years."

Coach asked, "Are you familiar with the term mentor?"

"Of course," responded Larry, "it is a person who helps you, like you and Miss Chris have with Sara and I."

Lesson: Find a Mentor; be a mentor

"The definition of a mentor is 'A wise and trusted counselor or teacher'. And yes, Chris and I have become your mentors. I suggest that you also find more mentors. We also suggest that you become mentors yourselves."

"Us?" Sara questioned.

"Sure. By definition, mentoring is a relationship between an experienced person and a less experienced person for the purpose of helping the individual with less experience learn and grow. Mentoring is a great way to serve people, and yourself. As each team member develop in knowledge and skills, the entire team's performance naturally improves. When that happens, everyone wins. And you'll find that YOU grow by mentoring, as well. As you reflect on your life experiences and distill them into nuggets to share with others, you *re-experience* the wisdom that's inside of you." Miss Chris offered and continued.

"If you position yourself to mentor others as we have, you will find that you can quickly become leaders. Keep in mind, great leaders are also great students; they are always learning."

Leadership

Coach continued. "And there is a big difference between a leader and a manager. A manager will help people see themselves as they are and help them incrementally; a leader will help people see themselves better than they are. Leaders are made, not born. This is contrary to the popular cliché. In my view, anyone can develop leadership skills and become a leader because leadership is the ability to influence others. Let's think about your workplace. There are those who are considered 'leaders' because of their position as a manager, supervisor, or administrator. Would you really follow these people if you didn't have to? You probably would not. You wouldn't because they are not truly leaders. Just because an individual has the title of a leader, does not mean that he or she exhibits the characteristics you would want to model to be an effective leader. Successful leadership begins with self-discipline and self-mastery, and yes this includes the financial arena. The most effective leaders are those who have chosen to develop the integrity, skills, knowledge, vision, attitude, and perspective required to inspire and encourage others to get to the next level. You can be a leader in any group, the home, workplace, church, ball team, or business. One of the problems I see in America today is that we put a big premium on management and not leadership."

"I see what you are saying Coach. At my workplace there are always management training programs. I started my career as a management trainee. I took management classes in college, I learned how to manage people, manage a budget, and manage a project. But no one ever taught me how to lead. Where does one go to learn that?" wondered Larry.

"That is a great question Larry! There is a relatively new concept that it being written about entitled the 'leadership vacuum'. As part of your growth process, I want you to do a little research about that. You will find writers looking at the subject in big business, politics, charities, and every other type of organization that you can imagine. It is my belief that everyone is a leader because all of us influence others to some degree. Most, however, haven't developed the skills to maximize the opportunities for themselves. John Maxwell, Chris Widener, Donald Trump, the US Marines, the US Army, Disney, Winston Churchill, Jack Welsh and many others have written about developing leadership principles, and I would recommend any of those resources."

Miss Chris suggested. "Before jumping into mentoring others, please keep the following in mind: All mentoring relationships need to focus on the people being mentored. Remember that it's not about you, it is about them. Accept them for who they are. Help them advance at their own pace."

She continued. "Secondly, avoid treating people you are mentoring as incompetent or incapable. Rather, think of them as individuals lacking in experience or valuable team members who need guidance. And never forget where YOU came from. Earlier in your career, you didn't know what you know now. Why should they?"

"Thirdly, don't criticize or belittle. Instead, help those you mentor to think through the consequences of their behavior and to identify more positive ways of handling difficult or troubling situations. And, by all means, hold the people you are mentoring responsible for their success. Be willing to give of yourself and your time, but insist that they do the same."

"I can appreciate that advice, Miss Chris. You and Coach have done that for us and followed your own advice. Thank you for that." Larry said graciously. "What else should we know about people?"

Lesson: Surround Yourself

"Another lesson we have learned is that you should surround yourself with good people. Webster defines surround as 'to enclose on all sides or to encompass.' One of the lessons that we have learned in life is this, surround on ALL sides, not only for financial help but also for emotional, physical, legal and all aspects of your life. The world is complicated and changing fast so you want to align yourselves with people with mutual best interests. It is unrealistic to believe that everyone is going to look out for your best interests above their own, but you can certainly find people with which you can align your interests for mutual benefits."

Lesson: People are focused on themselves

"For the most part people do things for themselves, not against you. People get confused about this all the time. Most people are focused on improving their situation not destroying yours."

Lesson: Learn to receive FEEDBACK

"One of the biggest values of surrounding yourself with good people is feedback. Our lives are filled with action, feedback, action, feedback etc. Let me give you a simple example. When you climb on a bathroom scale in the

127

morning and it says that you are 10 pounds overweight, is that good feedback or bad feedback?"

"It would be bad because no one wants to be overweight," replied Larry.

"Really?" asked Coach. "What if you were 20 pounds overweight a week before and now you are down to 10 pounds overweight? We have to look at the situation in the entire context. And that is the value of surrounding yourself with good people. Some actually create what they call 'accountability groups'. The point is that no man is an island and you need and want others to help you. Feedback from our trusted advisers is crucially important. It can be a very important source of information about us and our environment. The problem is, if we do not like the feedback, our subconscious minds may block it out, distort, diminish, or deny the importance of that information. One of the best examples of the importance of feedback I can share is that of being an athlete. During practice, the coach would frequently stop and point out, directly and passionately how we were doing something wrong, usually followed up with 'that will cost you a lap'. He would also point out situations when we did them correctly. This feedback was crucial for us improving as a team and developing our individual skills. What I see today, is that most people ignore the feedback or in a lot of cases don't even hear it, because the person attempting to give the feedback is trying to be politically correct and not hurt anyone's feelings, I think this is bologna. Personal coaches deal with accountability on a daily basis. They define accountability as first asking for observations, advice and direction and second, being willing to be humble enough to accept the feedback and remain teachable enough to apply it.

"When we talk about this Pillar of Success, I like to discuss a couple of historical figures and their impact on the people that they lead. You will recognize these leaders from the Bible.

Moses

"Moses was considered one of the great leaders in history. His style was very pragmatic. He was obviously very smart and wise as people brought him their problems constantly. He liberated the people from a tyrant and a very bad situation. He must have been pretty powerful because *everyone* followed. We do not read about any of the Israelites staying behind because they did not like him."

"His mission was to lead his people out of Egypt and to the promised land. This was obviously no easy task. Historians estimate the number of people in the tens, if not hundreds of thousands. Let's try to put ourselves in their place. Here is a guy named Moses that killed an Egyptian guard and years later goes to the Pharaoh and tells him that he must 'let my people go'," Coach mimicked the famous Charlton Heston portrayal of Moses from the Movie '*The Ten Commandments*'.

"You don't like your life here in Egypt because you are a slave, but you and your family have a roof over your head and food for your daily needs. Now Moses tells you and others that you are going to be leaving and walking across the desert until you get to the 'Promised Land'. I can hear them in my imagination saying 'yeah right'. Do you know where it is? How long will it take? How do you know life will be better? How about this milk and honey stuff? How are we going to eat? How long do we get to stay? Are you sure Pharaoh said it was okay? What is the weather like? Are there scorpions out there?

"It essentially came down to Moses convincing the people that the devil they knew was worse than the devil they didn't. He was passionate, confident, and focused. He convinced them that they were working toward something together. He convinced them that the future could be better than the past. He convinced them they did not need to view themselves as slaves anymore. Keep in mind that was the only life the people had ever known. Their parents and parents' parents had been slaves in Egypt for hundreds of years.

"After 40 years of walking in the dessert, another catastrophe happens. Moses dies. Now what?"

Joshua

"I am sure the people for the most part froze in fear. We then meet Joshua who steps forward and takes control of the situation and responds by telling the people that 'in three days, we are going in'. Again, put yourself in the shoes of the Israelite people. The questions would be fast and furious. Who put you in charge? Why do we have to go in three days, can't we properly grieve for Moses? Is the water cold? Are we moving too fast? Aren't there giants over there? Joshua became a great leader, in my opinion, because of the following key issues that I believe you and Sara need to develop in yourselves and also look for in your mentors."

Been there, done that

"The first key is that Joshua had been there before. As you may recall, years before, he went on mission to investigate the Promised Land with 11 of his fellow soldiers. He and Caleb were the only ones with a positive report; the others focused and reported on the giants. Joshua's confidence came from the fact that he had been there before and that is critical in your mentors and the people whom you seek advice."

Look at the Positive

"The second key issue is that Joshua and Caleb chose to look at the positive not the negative. People can easily get sucked down in to the muck. That is a life choice, do you want to be positive or negative? There is always challenges and issue and there always will be. That is not the question. The question is how you choose to view and deal with them. We covered this in detail when we talked about the 2nd Pillar, Perspective."

Break out of Status Quo

"The third key is that Joshua made demands on the peoples' lives. He didn't accept their excuses; he didn't buy into their problems. He didn't buy into their fear or their ignorance. He didn't accept the 'status quo' or the mentality 'we have always done it this way'. He assumed and acted on that assumption that the people could accomplish more. In my view every good leader does the same. Joshua encouraged people to take action that they may not have made without the encouragement. That is the essence of leadership."

"One final thought I would like to discuss regarding the 4th "P", People, is to suggest you learn to be abnormal. I know it is an unusual word and an unusual concept but let's discuss it. When I suggest abnormality what comes to your mind?"

"My first thought is being different or a bit different, maybe one who marches to the beat of a different drummer," replied Sara.

"My first thought is the scene from Young Frankenstein where Igor is sent to get a brain for the monster and finds one labeled *abnormal*, I laugh every time I think of that movie and that scene," Larry chuckled.

"Both are great thoughts! In order to be abnormal I think we need to try to define 'normal' and as I go through a list of what is *normal*, let's figure out if that is what you want at this time of your lives. Are you ready?"

"Absolutely," Sara and Larry both said.

"So let's look at what *normal* people do, think, and say specifically as it relates to money, career, and finances. I believe that what makes people normal or abnormal is primarily a function of the programming they receive. It is *normal* to receive a lot of programming from the school systems, our family, and our social circle. These institutions claim that it is *normal* to have a job, is that is *normal*? Well, the government enforces this belief with the terminology of being "unemployed" The press reports that the unemployment rate is 9.6%. That means that over 90% of Americans have jobs. I haven't had a job in over 25 years. I am not sure what category that puts me in, but clearly it is *abnormal*. *Normal* people will never be financially free or independent; they will rely on their employers, or the government for their day to day living. Again, statistics tell us that only about 1/3 of 1% has a net worth of $5 Million or more. So clearly it is abnormal to be wealthy. Obviously, it is easier in one sense to have a net worth of zero (15%) than to be wealthy. On the other hand, living at that level doesn't sound very easy to me.

"*Normal* people make less than $200,000/year and have little in the way of financial assets. As a matter of fact, most *normal* people are more concerned about their income as opposed to net worth and assets. They spend more time planning their vacations than they spend planning their financial future and spend more money on their monthly car payment than they spend on their financial education. *Normal* people look forward with great anticipation to getting a tax refund, *abnormal* people make sure they pay as little as possible. You stated before that you thought it was easier for me to say these things because we are already rich. What came first, being rich or planning and doing the things we have shared with you to become rich?" asked Coach.

Larry and Sara looked at each other and then back at Coach. Larry finally said "We have learned from you that planning comes first and then we see results. That was your experience and you are helping us do the same. It is hard to believe it is really this easy, to change our internal programming in order to obtain different results."

"As review let's share the stories of three contemporary people to illustrate how fear and normalcy can limit your financial futures. Have you heard of Ron Wayne, Larry Reinert, or Phil Knight?" asked Coach

"No, we haven't," replied Sara for both of them.

"Well, let's start with Ron Wayne's story. He was one of three founders of a company in 1976, serving as the venture's adult supervision. Wayne drew the first logo, wrote the three men's original partnership agreement, and wrote the first product manual. Wayne received a 10% stake in the company but relinquished his stock for $800 less than two weeks later, on April 12 1976.[9] The reason he did this, he has stated, is that legally all members of a partnership are personally responsible for any debts incurred by any partner and unlike his younger partners, Wayne had personal assets that potential creditors could seize. Later that year, venture capitalists developed a business plan and converted the partnership to a corporation. Wayne received another check for $1,500 for his agreement to forfeit any claims against the new company. In its first year of operations (1976), the company's sales reached $174,000. In 1977, sales rose to $2.7 million, in 1978 to $7.8 million, and in 1980 to $117 million. By 1982, the company had a billion dollars in annual sales. Wayne says that he did not regret selling the stock as he had made the 'best decision with the information available to me at the time.' Wayne also stated that he 'felt the enterprise would be successful, but at the same time there would be bumps along the way and I couldn't risk it. I had already had a rather unfortunate business experience before. I was getting too old and those two were whirlwinds. It was like having a tiger by the tail and I couldn't keep up with these guys'. If you haven't guessed yet, the company he founded was Apple and he sold his stock to Steve Jobs and Steve Wozniak. The one word to describe this is *oops*. What I find interesting about this story and the others I will share, is that hindsight is 20/20. We can all look back and call it a mistake, but what would YOU have done? Have you had opportunities that you missed? Maybe nothing on the scale of Apple but have you missed opportunities?

"The next story is about Larry Reinert. Larry is credited as one of the designers of GI Joe. As you may recall the development of G.I. Joe led to the coining of the term "action figure", an alternative for boys that did not want to be playing with dolls. Larry Reiner, who was then the head of the games division at Ideal Toys, reportedly had the option of taking his compensation in a lump sum or as a percentage of each sale. Larry chose the former which is estimated to have cost him tens of millions of dollars. Again, the lesson we can learn by looking at the situation with our 20/20 vision is choosing the *'normal'* path may not be the best option available.

"The final story is about Phil Knight. Phil and his partner Bill Bowerman started a company that was founded on January 25, 1964 as Blue Ribbon Sports. The company initially operated as a distributor for Japanese shoe maker Onitsuka Tiger (now ASICS), and most of their sales were at track meets, selling the product out of Knight's automobile.

"The company's first self-designed product was based on Bowerman's 'waffle' design. After the University of Oregon resurfaced the track at Hayward Field, Bowerman began experimenting with different out soles that would grip the new urethane track more effectively. His efforts were rewarded one Sunday morning when he poured liquid urethane into his wife's waffle iron. Bowerman developed and refined the so-called 'waffle' sole which would evolve into the now-iconic Waffle Trainer in 1974.

"By 1980, the company, with the 'abnormal' sole, had reached a 50% market share in the U.S. athletic shoe market, and the company went public in December of that year. Its growth was due largely to 'word-of-foot' advertising, to quote a print ad from the late 1970, rather than television ads. The company's first national television commercials ran in October 1982 during the broadcast of the New York Marathon. Over the years, being 'abnormal' they were often rejected as they sought professional athletes to be their spokesman. They were turned down by Isaiah Thomas, among others. They have been criticized for everything from their manufacturing practices to their advertising campaigns. And yet Phil Knight and Nike are now considered a world leader in a number of areas. His story is one that required persistence, patience, intestinal fortitude, and well, courage.

"And that is all I have for you today. Let's just enjoy the rest of the day with the great company, food and view, shall we?"

"That sounds great. We are so honored to get to meet you and learn so much. We are not sure how we can ever thank you," Sara replied. "Here is a small token of our appreciation." She handed them the picture.

Miss Chris thanked them and said "We told you that we do this for ourselves, just as much as for you. Now we have made new friends and we hope that we can continue meeting often."

"We'd like that," Larry spoke for both of them.

And with that they enjoyed the rest of the day by the ocean with their new friends."

QUESTIONS TO PONDER AND ACTIONS TO TAKE

If you make the average of your five closest friends, how does that make you feel?

Are there people that you would like to get to know? What are you doing to make that happen?

What are you doing to find ways to add value to other peoples' lives?

CHAPTER 8
NOW WHAT?

As Larry and Sara looked at each other, looked at their children and looked at the notebooks that they had created, they wanted to know if they had just lived through a dream. Were the 4P's really the secret? Did they really just spend some time with real people that had made it and made it big? Were they really *abnormal*? Were other families laying awake at night worrying about their financial futures? The thoughts swirled through their heads.

Sara broke the silence with the question: "Now what? It was great that we had the opportunity to meet with Miss Chris and Coach, but what do we do with all this information? I feel so overwhelmed but also encouraged and excited. For the first time, I feel like we are in control of our financial lives."

"I feel the same way," Larry agreed. "Now that we know, I feel like I am in control of the car. We have a road-map but can I really drive and get us there? What if I make the wrong turn? Or get us lost? Or broken down? I guess ignorance really is bliss, now that I know, I feel responsible and empowered. Before I felt like I was the doing the best I could and it was out of our control. That was the easy way, as I look at it now. To summarize Coach, my perspective has changed because I know some new principles. I know it won't be easy but neither is this way. Everything Coach and Miss Chris said makes sense. Now I guess it is up to us to implement and execute."

"Remember when Coach gave us the analogy of the 'success radio station'? I think we should commit to tuning in to that and only that station. We should teach the kids the 4Ps as soon as possible. I have an idea, why don't we compare our notebooks and create one for the family?" Sara offered.

"Great idea!" agreed Larry. "Let's start at the beginning. The very first thing I have in my notebook is that I AM responsible. I have to overcome my fear with action and my ignorance with knowledge. I also have a couple of notes to myself that I have to admit. I was skeptical the first time you mentioned Miss Chris. I mean, who do we know that would go out of their way to help us? But wow, was I wrong! I think it was Robert Frost that said 'I took the one less traveled by and that has made all the difference.' I am committed to that. Looking around, it seems that doing *normal* things ends badly in most cases. I made a lot of notes about action, but unlike before where I think I did things just to feel like I was making progress because I was moving; now I KNOW my actions have to have focus and intention. I also wrote that if everyone else is doing it, it is probably the wrong thing to do."

"I think that we just started our *Abnormal Journey!*" Larry and Sara stated in unison.

Footnotes

1. Source: http://jec.senate.gov/public/index.cfm?
   p=SubprimeMortgageCrisis
2. Source: Career Builder Survey , May-June 2010)
3. Source:
   http://articles.moneycentral.msn.com/Investing
   /Extra/USSavingsRateFallsToZero.aspx
4. Source: U.S. Department of Commerce
5. Source: CNN, NetWorth IQ, FRB: Federal
   Reserve.gov
6. Source:
   http://money.cnn.com/2010/05/03/news/econ
   omy/henrys_struggle.fortune/index.htm?
   source=cnn_bin&hpt=Sbin
7. Source: 'The Case Against Home Ownership'
   published in **TIME** magazine
8. Source AARP Bulletin 7/1/10
9. Source:
   http://en.wikipedia.org/wiki/Ronald_Wayne#cite
   _note-mercurynews-1#cite_note-mercurynews-1

17062311R00082

Made in the USA
Charleston, SC
24 January 2013